S0-BAI-318

Women of Achievement

Amelia Earhart

Women of Achievement

Abigail Adams

Jane Addams

Susan B. Anthony

Tyra Banks

Clara Barton

Nellie Bly

Julia Child

Hillary Rodham Clinton

Marie Curie

Ellen DeGeneres

Diana, Princess of Wales

Amelia Earhart

Tina Fey

Ruth Bader Ginsburg

Joan of Arc

Angelina Jolie

Helen Keller

Madonna

Michelle Obama

Sandra Day O'Connor

Georgia O'Keeffe

Nancy Pelosi

Rachael Ray

Anita Roddick

Eleanor Roosevelt

Martha Stewart

Barbara Walters

Venus and Serena Williams

Women of Achievement

Amelia Earhart

AVIATOR

Jeremy K. Brown

CHELSEA HOUSE
An Infobase Learning Company

AMELIA EARHART

Copyright © 2011 by Infobase Learning

All rights reserved. No part of this book may be reproduced or utilized in any form or by any means, electronic or mechanical, including photocopying, recording, or by any information storage or retrieval systems, without permission in writing from the publisher. For information, contact:

Chelsea House
An imprint of Infobase Learning
132 West 31st Street
New York, NY 10001

Library of Congress Cataloging-in-Publication Data
Brown, Jeremy K.
  Amelia Earhart : aviator / by Jeremy K. Brown.
    p. cm. — (Women of achievement)
  Includes bibliographical references and index.
  ISBN 978-1-60413-910-5 (hardcover : acid-free paper) 1. Earhart, Amelia, 1897–1937—Juvenile literature. 2. Women air pilots—United States—Biography—Juvenile literature. 3. Air pilots—United States—Biography—Juvenile literature. 4. Cross-country flying—History—20th century—Juvenile literature. 5. Flights around the world—History—20th century—Juvenile literature. I. Title.
  TL540.E3B746 2011
  629.13092—dc22
  [B]
                                    2011000037

Chelsea House books are available at special discounts when purchased in bulk quantities for businesses, associations, institutions, or sales promotions. Please call our Special Sales Department in New York at (212) 967-8800 or (800) 322-8755.

You can find Chelsea House on the World Wide Web at
http://www.infobaselearning.com.

Text design by Erik Lindstrom
Cover design by Ben Peterson and Alicia Post
Composition by EJB Publishing Services
Cover printed by Yurchak Printing, Landisville, Pa.
Book printed and bound by Yurchak Printing, Landisville, Pa.
Date printed: July 2011
Printed in the United States of America

10 9 8 7 6 5 4 3 2 1

This book is printed on acid-free paper.

All links and Web addresses were checked and verified to be correct at the time of publication. Because of the dynamic nature of the Web, some addresses and links may have changed since publication and may no longer be valid.

CONTENTS

On Howland Island

The red flags, lined neatly along the island's three runways, fluttered faintly in the tropical breeze, easily seen from the air. The native birds had been cleared, moved off the landing strips, forcibly in some cases. On the beaches and waters surrounding the small dot of land in the middle of the central Pacific Ocean, routine patrols were under way. In a tiny house, a bed sat, freshly made. All around, anticipation was in the air. Howland Island was expecting a guest.

This island was to be one of the last stopping points for Amelia Earhart, the world-famous pilot who was just days away from completing her historic around-the-world flight. For Earhart, already a legend in the world of aviation, it would be another achievement in a career filled with them.

Aviator Amelia Earhart helped to change the world's perception of what women could accomplish. In 1937, nine years after she became the first woman to fly across the Atlantic Ocean, Earhart set about to become the first female pilot to circle the globe.

Since 1928, when she had become the first woman to cross the Atlantic, Earhart had set about shattering the world's perspective on what women could achieve. Over the next nine years, Earhart continued to set numerous speed and distance records and became the first female pilot to fly solo across the Atlantic Ocean and the first woman to fly the Pacific Ocean.

HISTORY IN THE MAKING

Now, almost a full decade after first capturing the world's attention, Earhart was set to make history again by becoming the first female pilot to circumnavigate the globe. She needed to complete this landing, coming down in the middle of the ocean on a spot of land only slightly larger than a football field. It was a difficult and trying task, but one the world was certain she could accomplish.

Back in the United States, everyone waited eagerly for news of Earhart's journey. Fans had followed her from the first days of her flying career, when the press compared her to Charles Lindbergh, the famous pilot who had crossed the Atlantic Ocean in 1927, and called her "Lady Lindy." To the world, Earhart was their celebrity, a no-nonsense everyday gal who talked plainly and spoke her mind. Her straightforward demeanor and tomboyish good looks made her seem approachable, even relatable to the American public. They cheered her successes and waited to see what she had planned next.

Earhart came from humble beginnings, growing up in a small Kansas town, but she rose to incredible heights. Now Earhart was on the cusp of a flight that would cement her place in the annals of female pilots, and aviation overall, for all time. She needed only to make this landing, and the rest of the flight would go smoothly.

Aware of their place in this historic event, the men stationed on Howland Island, a U.S. territory, watched the skies and waited for the silver glimmer that would tell them that Earhart was on her way.

Beginnings

The skies over Atchison, Kansas, were gray and menacing on July 24, 1897, as an electrical storm erupted, breaking a heat wave that had gripped the tiny Midwestern town for several days. As the night wore on, the clouds burst and rain lashed the small white house on First Street where Amy Earhart, with her husband, Edwin, at her side, was about to give birth.

By 11:30 P.M., the storm had blown itself out, the night was calm and cool, and Amelia Mary Earhart had come into the world weighing a very healthy nine pounds (four kilograms).

Three months later, on the day of Amelia's baptism, the skies opened up yet again, releasing a torrent of rain that brought an end to a six-week drought. These unpredictable and rather unusual changes in the weather could be seen as omens for the wild and stormy life of Amelia Earhart.

CHILDHOOD

Even growing up, Amelia's life was an unconventional one. When she was three years old, Amelia was sent to live with her grandparents, Judge Alfred Otis and Amelia Otis in Atchison. Amelia's mother made this decision for several reasons. For starters, Amelia's grandmother was having a difficult time coping with the deaths of her son and his wife, as well as that of her mother, Maria Grace Harres. In addition, Amelia's grandfather, Judge Otis, had been suffering from mental illness and depression. In those days, such things were not often discussed, much less treated. And lastly, Amy Earhart had recently given birth to another daughter, Grace Muriel Earhart, and having two small children to care for with little help was proving difficult. As a result, Amelia spent most of the year in Atchison and summers with her parents 50 miles (80 kilometers) away in Kansas City.

Life in Atchison was idyllic for Amelia. The Otis family was a prominent one in town, and it seemed as though there was family everywhere. The town also spurred on

DID YOU KNOW?

Amelia Earhart's mother, born Amelia Otis in 1870, was an adventurous free spirit like her daughter. She holds the distinction of being the first woman ever to climb Pikes Peak, a 14,110-foot-high (4,300-meter-high) mountain in the Rocky Mountains of Colorado.

Amelia Earhart was born in 1897 in this home in Atchison, Kansas, which belonged to her grandparents, Judge Alfred Otis and Amelia Otis. When Amelia was three years old, she came to live with her grandparents.

Amelia's already-growing sense of adventure. Without her grandmother's knowledge, she would often go down to the butcher's shop, where the butcher, whose daughter was a friend of Amelia's, would let the girls ride his horses. She would also explore the caves along the Missouri River, even going so far as to put up signs that read "Beware" to keep other people out of her favorite ones.

When she was seven years old, Amelia went to the World's Fair in St. Louis, Missouri, with her family. While she enjoyed riding the Ferris wheel, she was upset that her mother didn't allow her to ride on the roller coaster. So, upon returning to Atchison, she decided to build her own. With the help of some friends, she put it together using a pair of two-by-fours propped against the roof of her grandfather's toolshed; the cart was a wooden box with roller skates for wheels. For the first ride, Amelia rocketed down the wooden boards and tumbled out onto her head as the cart came to a sudden stop. Unfazed, she added more wood to the track until the makeshift roller coaster was working perfectly.

Amelia was a playful, bold child who did not believe that girls should be limited from doing any of the activities that boys did. Attending the private College Preparatory School in Atchison, Amelia longed to play on the basketball team. Girls, however, were only allowed to be cheerleaders, rooting on the sidelines for the boys as they played. This did not sit well with Amelia, who promptly went up to the captain of the basketball team and asked him to teach her how to play. To everyone's surprise, he agreed. While it did not mean she was on the team, Amelia still learned enough to play ball with her friends in a nearby park.

During the winter, all the children in Atchison would gather for sledding down the hill on North Second Street. Tradition held that the boys lay down on their sleds, while the girls sat up straight. Amelia, however, owned a boys' model sled—given to her by her father—and rode down the hill lying flat on her stomach. Her defiance of the traditional feminine way of riding a sled once helped her to avoid a near disaster. On this occasion, when the hill was particularly icy, Amelia suddenly found herself in the path of a horse and cart. Because she was lying down, she was able to maneuver the sled so that it went right between the horse's legs.

A CHANGE OF LOCATION

In 1908, Amelia's father, Edwin, was offered a job with a rail company in Des Moines, Iowa. Edwin, a railroad lawyer, had long struggled with work and had tried to live up to the high expectations set by his father-in-law, who was one of the most prominent judges in Kansas. Although he was a generous man and a hard worker, Edwin Earhart had found it difficult to make ends meet financially. At one point, things had become so bad that he decided to give up law and become an inventor. Using his railroad experience, he created a holder to carry the signal flags that flew from a train's caboose, only to learn that someone else had invented

AMELIA AND MURIEL

Although they lived 50 miles (80 kilometers) apart for much of their early years, Amelia and her sister, Muriel, were nevertheless quite close. They had nicknames for each other (Amelia was "Millie," while Muriel was "Pidge," a name given to her by her father because she was pigeon-toed), and they used them even as adults. Whenever they were together, the two girls would explore the riverbanks and wilderness of Atchison, catching a variety of animals and insects and, on one memorable occasion, holding races with worms they had dug up. Like her older sister, Muriel was more of a tomboy in nature. So athletic and active were the two of them that their mother had them wear specially made pants called "bloomers," which allowed them more freedom to run and ride bikes than the standard frilly dresses worn by girls at the time. It was a defiance of convention that gave both girls the confidence that they could do what they wanted to do, regardless of their gender.

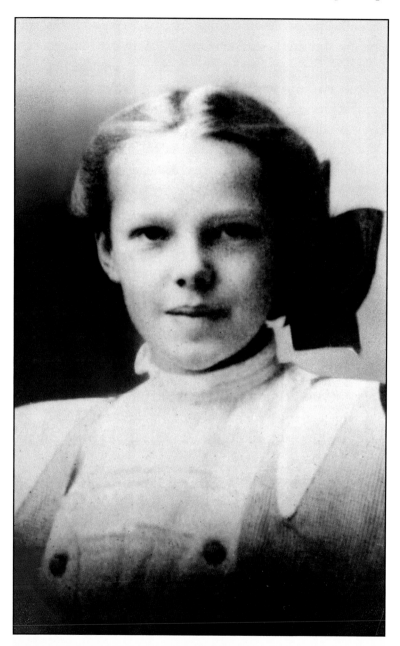

Even as a child, Amelia Earhart (shown here around age seven) believed that girls should not be excluded from doing what boys did. At school, she balked at being a cheerleader and instead asked the captain of the basketball team to show her how to play.

such a device two years before. After so many setbacks, this new job was a great opportunity for Edwin to provide for his family in the manner he intended.

Not wanting to disrupt Amelia's life in Atchison, Amy decided that she and Edwin would move to Des Moines while Amelia and Muriel would remain with her parents for a little while longer. Eventually, however, the family was reunited and began to live a comfortable and happy life in Iowa.

Edwin's new job came with certain benefits, such as free rail travel for the entire family. As a result, they took train trips together whenever they could. But these were no ordinary trips sandwiched in cars with other travelers. Because of the importance of Edwin's job, the family was able to travel in its own private car, which had a kitchen, a dining room, and even a personal butler to serve them.

Unfortunately, Edwin's troubles caught up with him. As before, he began to spend too much money and, to make matters worse, he began to drink as well. In time, Edwin's problems with alcohol would cost him his job.

Following her parents' deaths in 1912, Amelia's mother was due to inherit a substantial amount of money. The terms of her parents' wills, however, were such that Amy had no access to the funds. This was a direct result of Edwin's continued drinking troubles; Amy's parents had feared that Edwin would spend all of the inheritance on alcohol.

Drunk, out of work, and shunned by his family, Edwin Earhart eventually managed to gain an entry-level position as a railroad clerk in St. Paul, Minnesota, and moved the family with him.

Although Edwin continued to drink and disappoint his family with his behavior, Amelia tried to make the best of the situation. She studied hard in school, earning high grades, and played on the basketball team.

Eventually, Edwin relocated the family again, this time to Springfield, Missouri, where he believed he was to be hired as a claim agent. Upon arrival, however, he learned that the promised job did not exist. By this point, the strain on Amelia's mother had become too much, and the decision was made to move the family to Chicago to stay with friends while Edwin returned to St. Paul.

The difficult problems of her family life weighed very heavily on Amelia during her time in Chicago, and she became quieter and more withdrawn. For example, although the school she attended, Hyde Park High School, offered a top-notch athletic program, including coed sports and a girls' indoor baseball team, Amelia did not get involved in sports at all. In fact, she did not take part in any school activities. Instead, her day consisted of attending classes and

IN HER OWN WORDS

When Amelia Earhart spoke of her nomadic childhood as an adult, she did not hint at the troubles behind all the moves:

The family rolled around a good deal during my father's railroad years, Kansas City, Des Moines, St. Paul, Chicago—forward and back. What we missed in continuous contacts over a long period, we gained by becoming adapted to new surroundings quickly. I have never lived more than four years in any one place and always have to ask, "Which one?" when a stranger greets me by saying, "I'm from your home town."*

* Susan Butler, *East to the Dawn: The Life of Amelia Earhart.* Philadelphia: Da Capo Press, 1999, p. 69.

then going straight home to look after her mother, who had fallen ill as a result of the incredible stress of being married to Edwin Earhart.

Following her graduation from Hyde Park in June 1915, Amelia enrolled in the Ogontz School for Girls in Rydal, Pennsylvania, a small suburb just outside of Philadelphia. Here, traces of the old, vibrant Amelia Earhart resurfaced. Free from the burden of taking care of Amy, Amelia was able to indulge in her various interests. She played field hockey and excelled at the sport, so much so that she was invited to join Alpha Phi, an athletic sorority. Amelia also did well in her classes, earning high marks and even being made exempt from spelling classes after only two semesters.

DEFYING TRADITION

Around this time, Amelia began to think about what she wanted to do with her life. She had begun to compile a scrapbook entitled "Activities of Women," in which she pasted articles about various women who had unique and successful careers. Many of the jobs these women had were typically male-driven, such as a lookout for the U.S. Forest Service, a film producer, a police commissioner, and a lawyer from India. These women served as an inspiration to Amelia and reminded her that nothing could stand in the way of her dreams, whatever they may be.

Amelia continued to thrive at Ogontz, becoming vice president of her class, being asked to write the senior class song, and creating the class motto: "Honor Is the Foundation of Courage." Amelia also served as secretary for a local chapter of the Red Cross. In addition, she took part in a movement to disband secret societies, such as the sorority that she herself was a member of. The head of the school, Abby Sutherland, deemed these societies too exclusive and moved to dissolve them entirely. Amelia agreed and lobbied hard to ensure that these groups did break up. Her part in this cause made her somewhat unpopular for a time, but this did not bother Amelia. She was doing what she felt was right, and that was all that mattered to her.

That Christmas, she decided to travel to Toronto, Canada, and visit Muriel, who was attending St. Margaret's, a preparatory school. This visit would prove to be an important turning point in the life of Amelia Earhart—one that would help to set her on the path she would follow for the remainder of her days.

A Call to Action

By 1917, the nations of the world had been embroiled in a global conflict for three years. This conflict came to be known as World War I, though at the time it was referred to as simply the World War, the Great War, or the War to End All Wars.

World War I, which began in the summer of 1914, was a violent and bloody war that ultimately claimed more than 15 million lives, but for many people in the United States, its full impact was not felt. The United States did not enter the conflict until 1917, the same year that Amelia Earhart traveled to Toronto to visit her sister.

In Toronto, Amelia came face to face with the ravages of war. Although at Ogontz she had volunteered for the Red

Cross and knitted sweaters for the troops, in Toronto, she saw wounded Canadian troops firsthand walking the streets of the city. "There for the first time I realized what the World War meant," she later wrote. "Instead of new uniforms and brass bands, I saw only the results of four years' desperate struggle; men without arms and legs, men who were paralyzed, and men who were blind. One day I saw four one-legged men at once, walking as best they could down the street together."[1]

Following the Christmas holidays, Amelia returned to Ogontz but found that whatever motivation she had had to graduate had been replaced with a strong desire to help in the war effort. "Returning to school was impossible, if there was work that I could do,"[2] she said.

Although her decision did not entirely thrill her parents, Amelia knew that what she was doing was the right thing for her, and so she left Ogontz and returned to Toronto to find work as a nurse's aide. She enrolled in a first-aid course given by the St. John Ambulance Brigade's Voluntary Aid Detachment and upon graduating became what was known as a VAD.

AIDING THE WOUNDED

After graduation, Amelia briefly worked at the children's ward at Victoria Memorial Hospital before transferring to Spadina Military Hospital, where she took care of the patients who were suffering terrible emotional stress due to fighting in the war, a condition called "shell shock," though now commonly known as "combat stress reaction."

In the shell-shock ward, Amelia worked 12 hours a day, from seven in the morning until seven at night. In her book *20 Hrs., 40 Min.: Our Flight in the Friendship,* Amelia recalled her duties on the ward:

The headmistress at the Ogontz School for Girls had her students dress up in their graduation attire for Halloween. So even though Amelia Earhart donned her cap and gown, she did not graduate from Ogontz. Instead, she left school in her final year to work as a nurse's aide in Toronto, Canada, tending to soldiers wounded during World War I.

There were many beds to be made and trays and "nurishment" [sic] to be carried, and backs to be rubbed—some lovely ones!

Most of the men had been through a physical and emotional crisis. Many were not sick enough to be in bed and not well enough to find real occupation. Even when jobs were offered, many lacked the mental stamina to take them—or make good at them, if taken. Spiritually they were tired out. Generally speaking they were a far harder group to care for than the really sick. For with the latter the improvements noted by the patient from day to day are cheerful mile posts, while the poor lads had lost even that means of happiness.[3]

On her off days, Amelia and her sister enjoyed a full and active life, as they always had. They lived together in an apartment in Toronto's St. Regis hotel and often spent time horseback riding. Amelia's horse was named Dynamite, and it was her taming of this wild stallion that helped pave the way for her future career.

A trio of air force officers, impressed with how well she handled the short-tempered horse, invited her to a local airfield to watch them fly. Amelia agreed, and instantly became enamored with airplanes. "Though I had seen one or two at county fairs before, I now saw many of them, as the officers were trained at the various fields around the city," she later recalled. "Of course, no civilian had a chance of going up. But I hung around in my spare time and absorbed all I could. I remember the sting of the snow on my face when it was blown back from the propellers when the training plane took off on skis."[4]

From that point on, Amelia spent as much time as she could at the airfield, talking with the pilots and learning all there was to know about flying. On one occasion, at an air show, Amelia had a hair-raising encounter with an airplane that would have scared most people off of them for good. While standing in an open field watching a stunt flier, Amelia and a friend looked on as the pilot began to dive toward the crowd. Amelia remembered:

> He was bored. He had looped and rolled and spun and finished his little bag of tricks, and there was nothing left to do but watch the people on the ground running as he swooped close to them. . . . I remember the mingled fear and pleasure which surged over me as I watched that small plane at the top of its earthward swoop. Commonsense told me if something went wrong with the mechanism, or if the pilot lost control, he, the airplane and I would be rolled up in a ball together. I did not understand it at the time, but I believe that little red airplane said something to me as it swished by.[5]

IN HER OWN WORDS

In her book, *20 Hrs., 40 Min.*, Amelia Earhart describes the impact her visits to the Toronto airfield had on her:

> I have even forgotten the names of the men I knew then. But the memory of the planes remains clearly and the sense of the inevitability of flying. It has always seemed to me one of the few worthwhile things that emerged from the misery of war.[*]

[*] Amelia Earhart, *20 Hrs., 40 Min: Our Flight in the Friendship.* Washington, D.C.: National Geographic Society, 2003, p. 8.

That winter, Canada was struck by the Spanish flu epidemic that was spreading around the world, and Amelia soon fell ill. In those days, physicians did not have the advanced medicine they have today to treat illnesses. Antibiotics did not enter mainstream medicine until after Alexander Fleming's discovery of penicillin in 1928 and its development as a drug in the 1940s. As a result, Amelia was forced to undergo a painful operation to drain the infection from her sinuses.

While recovering from her sickness, Amelia left Toronto and went to Northampton, Massachusetts, to be with her mother and sister. Muriel had transferred to Miss Capen's School in Northampton, and Amy had moved there to be closer to her.

Amelia moved into Muriel's apartment but did not spend her convalescence idly. She took a course in automotive mechanics, teaching female ambulance drivers how to repair their engines. This course would prove very useful later in life, helping Amelia to understand how engines worked. She also learned to play the banjo, practicing on a used model she had purchased in a pawnshop for $25.

Her recovery gave Amelia time to think about her future. Eventually, inspired by her time as a nurse, she decided to take the next logical step and become a doctor. That fall, she enrolled in Columbia University and moved to New York City. "I had acquired a yen for medicine and I planned to fit myself for such a career,"[6] she later said.

LIFE IN NEW YORK

Amelia's time at Columbia was brief, but she managed to accomplish a lot while there, studying hard and earning a B-plus average. She also took advantage of living in New York City, attending concerts and riding horses in Central Park. She made waves at the school for her mischievous and daring ways. Perhaps the most famous example of this was her climbing of the great dome at the university, the highest point on campus. She and her friend Louise de Schweinitz (who had accompanied Amelia on other adventures around the college, such as exploring the tunnels and passages

AIR SHOWS

When Amelia Earhart first became interested in airplanes, air travel was still very much in its infancy. The Wright Brothers had made their famous first flight at Kitty Hawk, North Carolina, only 15 years earlier, and planes were very much a source of curiosity for the general public. In the wake of World War I, in which airplanes played a pivotal role, aviation was shifting from novelty item to full-blown attraction. It was then that air shows first started to, quite literally, take flight.

Air shows began around 1909 as aviation became more and more advanced, and they featured everything from aircraft on display to incredible feats of daring from the pilots themselves. Almost as soon as planes took to the sky, pilots were figuring out how best to put them through their paces, performing loops and barrel rolls and executing steep dives to thrill the crowds. Such pilots were said to be "barnstorming," and troupes of barnstormers traveled from town to town in what came to be called "flying circuses."

Besides the aerial acrobatics on display, air shows also featured daredevil stunts from the pilots, who would often leave their cockpits to walk, dance, and even play tennis on the wings of their aircraft.

Air shows continue today, and with the advent of jet flight and helicopters, they are more thrilling and sophisticated than

beneath the campus) managed to get the key to the narrow staircase that led to the dome's top, then climbed out onto it and basked in the spring sun as onlookers applauded.

After her first year at Columbia, Amelia suddenly decided to leave the school. She had come to realize that

A wing walker performed a stunt during an early air show in the skies over New Jersey. As advances in aviation were made throughout the early twentieth century, air shows became more and more popular across the United States.

ever. To find an air show in your area, check out http://www.airshow.com.

becoming a physician was not the career path she wanted for herself. "Scholastically I think I could have qualified," she observed, "but after a year of study I convinced myself that some of my abilities did not measure up to the requirements which I felt a physician should have."[7]

Another factor that led Amelia to leave medical school was her parents' decision to move to California in a last-ditch effort to reconcile their marriage. Edwin had ceased drinking, presumably for good this time, and had opened his own legal practice in Los Angeles. However, years of bad decisions and broken promises haunted Amy, and she found it hard to trust her husband as she once had. With that in mind, she invited her daughters to join them on the West Coast. Amelia, for one, was not altogether pleased with the idea of moving out west, but she agreed to do so for her parents' sake. As she left behind her sister, who was now attending Smith College in Northampton, Amelia let her know exactly how she felt about the situation, saying, "I'll see what I can do to keep Mother and Dad together, Pidge, but after that I'm going to come back here and live my own life."[8]

As it turned out, the move to California would prove to be the most important one of Amelia's life.

First Flight

In the early 1920s, aviation fever was gripping America. In the wake of World War I, planes and the pilots who flew them were romanticized in books and movies.

California was fast becoming the epicenter of aviation in the twenties. With its abundance of flat, dry land and its temperate climate, the conditions were perfect for flying, and residents wasted no time in taking advantage.

Shortly after her arrival on the West Coast, Amelia Earhart attended an air meet at Daugherty Field near Long Beach, California. Seeing the planes stretched out on the field under a clear-blue sky, Earhart knew right away that she wanted to become a pilot. She turned to her father, who did not seem to be enjoying the day as much as she was, and told him of her intentions to fly. Her father, though somewhat taken aback, was agreeable. He spoke to one of the officials at the meet and made arrangements for his daughter to go up in a trial flight the next morning.

Earhart arrived on the field promptly the next morning for her flight. Given that she was a woman, two pilots went up with her—one to fly the plane and one to catch her in case she became hysterical and decided to jump out. Such thinking was typical of the time period, but Earhart had been around planes before and was not at all nervous. Writing about the experience in *20 Hrs., 40 Min.*, she recalled that first flight:

> The familiar "contact" was spoken and the motor came to life. I suppose there must be emotion with all new experiences, but I can't remember any but a feeling of interest on this occasion. The noise of the motor seemed very loud—I think it seems so to most people on their first flight.
>
> The plane rose quickly over some nearby oil derricks which are part of the flora in Southern California. I was surprised to be able to see the sea after a few moments of climbing. At 2,000 feet [610 meters] the pilot idled the motor and called out the altitude for me. The sensation of speed is of course absent, and I had no idea of the duration of the hop. When descent was made I know the field looked totally unfamiliar. I could not have picked it out from among the hundreds of little squares into which populated areas are divided. One of the senses which must be developed in flying is an acuteness in recognizing characteristics of the terrain, a sense seldom possessed by a novice.[1]

HOOKED ON FLYING

When she came back down to Earth, Earhart's mind was made up, and the direction the rest of her life would take was chosen. She was going to learn to be a pilot. And she told her family as much upon returning home. "'I think I'd like to fly,' I told the family casually that evening," she recalled, "knowing full well I'd die if I didn't. 'Not a bad idea,' said my father equally casually. 'When do you start?'"[2]

Although Earhart was eager to begin flying lessons, a couple of obstacles were in the way. For starters, lessons were very expensive, costing around $500 for 12 hours. Since her father could not afford the lessons, Earhart agreed to secure a job to pay for them herself.

The second hurdle was finding the right instructor. Earhart did not particularly like the attitudes of some of the male instructors she had met and felt that she might learn better from a woman, who would understand some of the resistance aspiring female pilots encountered. That woman was 24-year-old Anita "Neta" Snook.

The first woman ever to graduate from the Curtiss School of Aviation, Snook was a pilot from Iowa who had moved to California so she could fly year-round. During the war, she had become notorious for her efforts to join the U.S. Army's military aviation service. When those efforts were not successful, she spent the war checking airplane engines for the British War Mission.

Snook and Earhart were very similar in their interests, their demeanor, and their defiance of conventions. Writing about Snook's appearance, one of her peers once wrote, "We were not quite sure as to whether Snooky was a man or a woman, as few of us ever saw her except in a pair of dirty coveralls, her reddish hair closely cropped, and her freckled face usually made up with the assistance of airport dust and a dash of grease."[3]

In December 1920, Earhart arrived at Kinner airport in Glendale, California, in search of Neta Snook. Snook, who was climbing into her Canadian Canuck airplane, recalled first seeing Amelia and Edwin approaching her:

Amelia Earhart began to take flying lessons in January 1921, receiving her first instruction from female aviator Neta Snook. Dismayed by the attitudes of male instructors, Earhart thought she might learn better from a woman. Here, Earhart appears next to a McLintic biplane in the early 1920s.

She was wearing a brown suit, plain but of good cut. Her hair was braided and neatly coiled around her head; there was a light scarf around her neck and she carried gloves. She would have stood out in any crowd and she reminded me of the well-groomed and cultured young ladies at the Frances Shimer Academy back in Mount Carroll, Illinois, my child-hood home. The gentleman with her was slightly gray at the temples and wore a blue serge business suit. He walked erect with a firm step.

"I'm Amelia Earhart and this is my father. I see you are busy, but could I have a few words with you? I want to learn to fly and I understand you teach students. . . . Will you teach me?"[4]

Snook agreed to take Earhart on as a student, informing her that the charge was $1 for every minute they were in the air. Earhart agreed to the rate, offering to pay with Liberty Bonds she had bought during the war.

On January 3, 1921, Earhart arrived at the airfield for her first lesson. In keeping with her character, she brought with her a book on aerodynamics. This was the first of many books she was to be seen carrying tucked under her arm. In fact, Snook later recalled seeing her with a book at all times.

Earhart's lessons began not in the air, but on the ground, with instruction on the basics of flying and the ins and outs of how planes worked. In time, though, Earhart got off the tarmac to do some flying of her own, albeit with a little assistance from Snook. "New students were instructed in planes with dual controls," Earhart explained. "The rudder and stick in the front of the cockpit are connected with those in the rear so that any false move the student makes can be corrected by the instructor. Every move is duplicated and can be felt by both fliers. One lands, takes off, turns, all with an experienced companion in command."[5]

Earhart took to flying quite well, although a couple of mishaps occurred along the way. "Crashes were frequent enough in these earlier days," she wrote. "I had one myself, during my instruction period. Owing to carelessness in not refueling, the motor cut out on the takeoff, when the plane was about 40 or 50 feet [12 to 15 meters] in the air. Neta Snook was with me, but she couldn't help depositing us in a cabbage patch nearby. The propeller and landing gear suffered and I bit my tongue."[6] Nevertheless, she regained her composure and faced the situation with her trademark humor. Snook recalled how, immediately after the plane had struck the ground, she turned around and saw Earhart powdering her nose and saying, "We have to look nice when the reporters come."[7]

IN HER OWN WORDS

Amelia Earhart had this to say about what was driving her to learn to fly:

> Whether it was considered the thing to do or not was irrelevant. As a little girl I had ridden my buggy in the stable; I had once climbed up on a delivery horse; I had explored the fearsome caves in the cliffs overlooking the Missouri; I had invented a trap and caught a chicken; I had jumped over a fence that no boy my age had dared to jump; and I knew there was more fun and excitement in life than I would have time to enjoy.*

* Mary S. Lovell, *The Sound of Wings: The Life of Amelia Earhart.* New York: St. Martin's Press, 1989, p. 41.

HER OWN PLANE

Nevertheless, despite such bumps in the road, Earhart's flying lessons were coming along, so much so that, after six months of training, on her twenty-fourth birthday, she laid out $2,000 to purchase her own plane, a yellow Kinner Airster that she dubbed *The Canary*. To help pay for the plane, Earhart landed a job at a telephone company, working in the mailroom. "I was associated with the office boys at the back of the office, an association which I was told was one of the worst in the organization. We did things to the mail, opened it, sorted it, distributed it. I also filed letters and then tried to find them again. I liked the job and the boys, who were very funny and not the criminals they were pictured."[8]

As Earhart progressed in her training, she began to take on the look of a pilot. She purchased a leather flying jacket, which she slept in and "aged" to give it the well-worn look of the jackets worn by the other fliers at the airfield. She also began to cut her waist-length hair into the short bob she would become famous for. Earhart did this slowly, cutting off only a little every few weeks, so as not to shock her mother too greatly.

Although she was fitting in well at the airfield and had logged a decent number of hours in the air, she felt she was still not ready for a solo flight. "I refused to fly alone until I knew some stunting," she said. "It seemed foolhardy to try to go up alone without the ability to recognize and recover quickly from any position the plane might assume, a reaction only possible with practice. In short, to become thoroughly at home in the air, stunting is as necessary as, and comparable to, the ability to drive an automobile in traffic."[9]

Eager to push herself further, Earhart parted ways with Snook as her instructor and began to fly with a man named John Montijo, an ex-army pilot who had flown in World War I and had recently come to Los Angeles to make a living by flying.

Under Montijo's instruction, Earhart learned the basics of stunt flying: banks, turns, barrel rolls, and loops. "I was then introduced to aerobatics and felt not a bit afraid when sent 'upstairs' alone for the first time."[10]

FIRST SOLO FLIGHT

Although she felt no fear and had hours of training to boost her confidence, Earhart's first solo flight almost did not get off the ground. Shortly after starting the plane, as she was taxiing down the runway, a shock absorber broke off, causing the aircraft's left wing to sag. "I didn't know just what had happened, but I did know something was wrong and wondered what I had done," she recalled. "The mental agony of starting the plane had just been gone through and I was suddenly faced with the agony of stopping it. It was all in a matter of seconds, of course, and somehow I contrived to do the proper thing. My brief 'penguin' flight came to a prompt conclusion without further mishap."[11]

Following her unfortunate takeoff, Earhart managed to repair her aircraft and get it off the ground, flying up to approximately 5,000 feet (1,500 meters) before making what she deemed to be a "thoroughly rotten landing."[12]

Rotten landing or not, Earhart was now flying solo, and the world of aviation was about to meet its newest and brightest star.

Grounded

By the start of 1922, Amelia Earhart was racking up hours in flight time and honing her skills. She was also earning a reputation around the airfield, with the aviation publication *The Ace* running articles about her exploits in the air. With Neta Snook having left Los Angeles to get married and start a family, Earhart was now the airfield's sole female flier, and the papers took notice. Articles cropped up in the *Los Angeles Times* and other publications, featuring half-page photos of Earhart clad in her flying gear and posing in front of her Airster. Even Bert Kinner, who had sold Earhart her plane, took advantage of her new celebrity, advertising his planes as "A lady's plane as well as a man's."

On October 22, 1922, Earhart climbed into her Airster with the intent to, as she put it, "establish its ceiling—that is, to see how high it would go."[1] As she further explained, there is a limit to how high a plane can go, and Earhart was eager to test that limit.

In the interest of making her flight a matter of official record, Earhart contacted the Aero Club of Southern California, asking it to seal her barograph. The barograph is a device that uses barometric pressure to record a plane's altitude. On a paper chart, rotated by clockwork, the barograph records in ink how high an aircraft is flying. Once it is sealed, the pilot cannot make alterations to it.

Higher and higher her aircraft climbed, reaching 13,000 feet (3,962 meters) with little difficulty. "Thereafter I began to have trouble," Earhart later said. "My spark control lever became disconnected and I could not regulate the spark in my engine. As a result, a terrific vibration and knocking started. I thought the engine would jump out of its frame. There wasn't anything to do but come down, although I was still climbing 50 feet [15 meters] a minute."[2]

When she touched ground, Earhart was shocked to learn that, engine trouble or not, she had reached 14,000 feet (4,267 meters), setting a new altitude record for women's flight. No woman pilot before her had ever flown so high.

Although her record was broken only a few weeks later by another female pilot, Ruth Nichols, the achievement fueled the fire of Earhart's ambition. She knew that she was on the right path in becoming a pilot, and she was determined to continue pushing the envelope. Almost immediately after setting the altitude record, Earhart climbed back into her plane and tried to fly even higher. This time, when she reached 12,000 feet (3,657 meters), Earhart found herself engulfed by a blanket of thick, dense fog. "This was an entirely new experience," she wrote, "and very disquieting. For the first time in my life, I had that strange feeling experienced by the flier in fog."[3]

Surrounded by fog, Earhart could not tell whether she was going up or down or even whether she was right side up.

Completely turned around and comparatively blind, Earhart had no choice but to put the plane in a tailspin and swoop down to 3,000 feet (914 meters) to get her bearings.

When she touched down, she learned that she had not broken her own record, but she took a lot away from the experience. By relying on her instruments as much as her eyesight, Earhart could gain a better sense of where she was in the sky and, in the event of unforeseen situations such as fog, be better prepared to handle them. It was an important step for her in her burgeoning aviation career.

CHANGE OF FORTUNE

Just as her career was taking off, however, the Earhart family's fortunes were dwindling, with Amy Earhart's inheritance having been reduced to a mere $20,000. In an effort to turn their situation around, Amy and Edwin invested, at Amelia's suggestion, in a gypsum mine in Nevada. This investment proved to be a disastrous one, as the mine was washed out in a flash flood.

With the money situation growing more and more dire, Amy had decided to take in boarders to help with the finances. One boarder was a young man named Sam Chapman. Sam and Amelia were about the same age and shared many of the same interests. On one occasion, they attended a meeting of the Industrial Workers of the World, an organization with socialist ties. The meeting, in which the topic of pensions for everyone over 60 was discussed, was broken up by the police, a fact that irritated Earhart. "Pensions are surely better than the poorhouse at sixty," she said. "I think the government ought to make people save some of their wages and give it back to them when they are old . . . [and] I think we should have had the right to talk it out tonight instead of being sent home like naughty children."[4]

The following spring, on May 16, 1923, Earhart received her flying certificate from the Fédération Aéronautique

Internationale, which would allow her to legally make attempts at breaking FAI records. Shortly afterward, she sold her airplane and began to look for a job that might help out with her family's money situation. Eventually, she found work at a commercial photography studio, mostly working in the darkroom developing photographs. When that company went under, Earhart decided to start her own photography business. This, too, never amounted to much, although she did capture a shot of an oil well gushing and sold the picture to a real estate developer, who used it in his advertising.

Eventually, Earhart purchased a new plane—most likely with help from Bert Kinner, who no doubt felt indebted to the publicity his airplanes received thanks to Earhart, as she could not afford to buy it outright. Nevertheless, Earhart continued to fly whenever she could. Unfortunately, in 1924, her sinus infection flared up again, requiring a second surgery to drain her sinuses. The surgery cost $500, which Earhart could not afford to pay. Eventually, the debt went to a collection agency, and it took her a full year to pay the money back.

At the same time, her parents, after years of trying to salvage their marriage, finally divorced. Amy was eager to leave California and start a new life, and Amelia, unemployed and recovering from surgery, opted to leave with her. She had hoped to make the journey by air, but expenses and her condition made that impossible. So, that summer, she sold her second airplane and purchased a Kissel automobile, which she christened "The Kizzle" or "The Yellow Peril," the latter a nod to its bright coat of paint.

The leisurely cross-country drive took Earhart and her mother 7,000 miles (11,265 kilometers) to Boston, with stops in Canada, Oregon, and Wyoming. By the time they reached Boston, the yellow automobile was covered in stickers from all the places the two women had visited. Everyone wanted to hear about their travels, as driving across the country in 1924 was still considered unusual.

Just three days after her arrival in Boston, Earhart checked herself into Massachusetts General Hospital for another sinus surgery. This time, a small fragment of bone was removed to assist in the drainage.

After recovering from her surgery, Earhart traveled to New York, where she lived with an old friend, Marian Stabler, on Long Island before returning to Columbia University in February 1925. The divorce, the cross-country trip, and the surgery had all but exhausted the family funds, so Earhart had little to no money most of the time.

Eventually, her money problems became such that Earhart was forced to withdraw from Columbia, having taken only two courses, physics and algebra. In algebra, she received a C-, which meant that she did not receive credit for the course. That summer, having returned to Boston, Earhart enrolled at Harvard summer school to take a math course and gain the credits she missed. This time she received an A for her work.

SOCIAL WORK

In 1925, desperate for money and unable to find any steady work in aviation, Earhart took a job as a social worker at Denison House, a settlement house in Boston designed to provide educational and social opportunities to the poor people of the city. There she taught English to local immigrants. Shortly after starting her new job, Earhart began the Syrian Mothers Club, an organization devoted to the Syrian immigrants in her classes, many of whom had children attending Denison House's kindergarten.

Earhart flourished at Denison House, taking children to the hospital in her bright yellow car and forming clubs, one of which was a basketball team composed of Chinese girls. The team proved talented enough to play a game against another settlement house from New York City.

While living in Boston, Amelia Earhart took a job as a social worker at Denison House, a settlement house that provided social and education programs for the city's poor. She continued to pursue aviation and is seen here in a training plane in 1926.

By 1928, Earhart had moved into Denison House and had become a director there. In addition, she was named a delegate to the Conference of the National Federation of Settlements in Boston, where she impressed all in attendance with her knowledge and insight into the field of social work.

In the midst of her success at Denison House, Earhart continued to find outlets for her love of flying. In May 1927, she flew over Boston and scattered free passes to a Memorial Day weekend carnival for the benefit of Denison House, an act that made headlines in the local papers.

Around this time, a Massachusetts architect by the name of Harold Dennison expressed interest in building an airport in New England. He reached out to an old friend, Bert Kinner, in California for help in getting his project under way. Kinner, who had kept in contact with Earhart ever since she left the West Coast, suggested that Dennison contact her as well. Dennison did so, and while Earhart did not have money to invest in the airfield, Dennison was still impressed enough to offer her a position with his new company. She accepted, while continuing to live and work at Denison House.

Among her various jobs aiding Dennison's project was interior decoration. Writing a letter to her old friend Marian Stabler, Earhart reported:

> The field opens on Tuesday next for flying in full force. I am having a great time selecting hangings and furniture for the main hangar. I certainly wish I had you here to consult as the thing will approach the bizazz (Heavens, I am trying to write bizarre) as the colors are orange, black, and blue, with a few spots of lavender and green thrown in.[5]

During this time, Earhart continued to make the papers for her flying and even managed to contribute an article about women and flying to the *Bostonian*, a publication that catered to the upper crust of Boston society. Earhart's article, titled "When Women Go Aloft," ran in the May issue and showcased her hope that someday there would be more women in the air. "While women are hopelessly adventurous, they seem content to take their thrills vicariously, and watch men do things a long time before they attempt to do them. I have hope that this year will see many more women flying."[6]

Meanwhile, unbeknownst to Earhart, events were unfolding that would ultimately launch her into the history books. On May 21, 1927, pioneering American aviator Charles Lindbergh landed at Le Bourget Airport in France after taking off from Roosevelt Field on New York's Long Island, completing the world's first solo transatlantic flight.

Lindbergh's success inspired people the world over, and it was not long before other aviators were seeking to rival his great accomplishment. A great number of fliers tried to match or surpass Lindbergh's feat, including five women. Of the five, three were killed, one's plane never got off the ground, and the other was rescued at sea.

CROSSING THE ATLANTIC

For a time, it seemed that Amy Phipps Guest, a wealthy American heiress who was the wife of Frederick E. Guest, an esteemed British politician and cousin to future British prime minister Winston Churchill, would make the flight, though as a passenger, not a pilot. She contacted Commander Richard E. Byrd, the famous aviator and adventurer who had attempted the transatlantic crossing in 1927 and would later gain fame as the first man to reach the South Pole by plane. Byrd agreed to supply an airplane, a converted Fokker seaplane that Phipps Guest dubbed *Friendship*.

As the time of the flight drew near, however, Phipps Guest's family intervened and demanded that she not go. Given the track record of the previous women who had made the flight, they all felt that Phipps Guest was courting death should she attempt to go. The heiress relented, but remained in charge of the expedition. "Keep my ship," she told the family lawyer. "I am determined an American shall be the first woman to fly across to England. Find me someone. Someone nice who will do us proud. I shall pay the bills."[7]

Charles Lindbergh became a national celebrity after he flew solo across the Atlantic Ocean in 1927 in his plane, *The Spirit of St. Louis*. His success inspired others to feats in the sky, including heiress Amy Phipps Guest, who was determined that an American would be the first woman to cross the Atlantic.

At the same time, New York publisher George Palmer Putnam, who had just published Lindbergh's book *We*, was investigating the Phipps Guest flight. He had received a tip that Richard Byrd had sold an airplane to a woman planning on traveling the Atlantic and, having worked with Byrd on his book *Skyward*, Putnam was instantly curious. He contacted Hilton H. Railey, a close friend who lived in Boston, and asked him to find out what he could.

Railey learned that a flight was indeed planned and that the woman in question was being represented by a lawyer named David T. Layman. Immediately, Putnam picked up the phone and contacted Layman, who told him that Phipps Guest was out and that the search for a replacement was under way. Putnam then got back to Railey, asking him to seek out a suitable candidate. Railey placed a call to Reginald R. Belknap, a rear admiral who was well connected in Boston aviation circles. Belknap informed Railey that he did know someone who might fit the bill, "a social worker who flies," as he described her. "Call Denison House and ask for Amelia Earhart."[8]

On April 7, 1928, Earhart received a phone call that would change the course of her life forever. Writing in her

CHARLES LINDBERGH

Born in Detroit, Michigan, on February 4, 1902, Charles Lindbergh was fascinated with aviation from an early age and began to fly when he was only 20 years old. In 1927, he made the first-ever solo flight across the Atlantic Ocean in his plane, *The Spirit of St. Louis*. The flight was inspired by New York City hotelier Raymond Orteig, who offered $25,000 to the first aviator who could complete the flight. Lindbergh's flight made him a national celebrity and a hero to would-be pilots everywhere. Five years after his flight, Lindbergh again made headlines when his son, Charles Jr., was kidnapped and murdered near the family's home in New Jersey. Following the tragedy, Lindbergh escaped from public life to Europe and worked on inventing, creating the world's first artificial heart in 1935. After flying more than 50 combat missions as a civilian consultant in World War II, Lindbergh retired to Hawaii, where he spent the remainder of his years. In 1954, he won the Pulitzer Prize for his book, *The Spirit of St. Louis*. In 1974, following a battle with lymphoma, Lindbergh passed away at the age of 72.

book *20 Hrs., 40 Min.*, she recalled what happened that day in detail:

> I was working as usual around Denison House. The neighborhood was just piling in for games and classes and I was as busy as could be. I remember when called to the phone I replied I couldn't answer unless the message was more important than entertaining many little Chinese and Syrian children. The word came assuring me it was.
>
> I excused myself and went to listen to a man's voice ask me whether I was interested in doing something aeronautic which might be hazardous. At first I thought the conversation was a joke, and told the gentleman so. At least twice before I had been approached by bootleggers who promised rich reward and no danger—"absolutely no danger to you, Leddy."
>
> The frank admission of risk piqued my curiosity and I enquired how and why I had been called.
>
> I demanded references and got them. They were good references, too. After checking up, I made an appointment for late the same day.
>
> "Should you like to fly the Atlantic?"
>
> Such was the greeting when I met Hilton H. Railey, who had done the telephoning.[9]

And just like that, Earhart was about to make the quantum leap from unknown social worker to world-famous aviatrix. Her time in the spotlight had arrived.

Flight of the
Friendship

Shortly after receiving that fateful phone call, Amelia Earhart found herself traveling to New York City to meet with George Putnam and David Layman. Earhart's poise and confidence impressed both men.

Her self-assurance won her interviewers over and, after a series of background checks, Earhart was offered the position. She would not be paid for her work, however, and any money she received from speaking engagements or book contracts would be returned to Amy Phipps Guest to help pay for the flight. Regardless of the terms, Earhart's mind was made up. "Under the circumstances there was only one answer," she said. "I couldn't say no."[1]

Earhart was named "commander" of the flight, and while pilot Wilmer Stultz and copilot Louis Gordon would fly the plane, it was agreed that Earhart would have some time at the controls, if only to help bolster the story of a woman flying the Atlantic.

Not long after her acceptance, Earhart traveled to East Boston to the hangar where the *Friendship* was kept. When she first laid eyes on it, the plane was being outfitted with pontoons to ensure greater safety in the event of a water landing. It was also being given a coat of reddish-orange paint, which would make it much easier to spot in the ocean, should such an emergency arise.

A LOW PROFILE

Amid all the preparations, Earhart was told to keep quiet regarding all matters related to the flight. If word got out that such a journey was in the works, media and public curiosity would be so intense as to possibly jeopardize the flight. So, for the next several weeks, Earhart kept a low profile. Gloomy weather prevented the plane from taking off in mid-May, as had been the original plan, and so everyone was forced to wait it out. "I have a memory of long gray days which had a way of dampening our spirits against our best efforts to be cheerful," she wrote. "We tried to be casual by keeping occupied."[2] She continued to work at Denison House, took drives in her yellow Kissel, flew when she could, and spoke to almost no one about the *Friendship*, although she did inform Marion Perkins at Denison House, asking her for a two-week leave of absence from work.

During her downtime while awaiting the flight, Earhart also began to spend time with George Putnam and the crew of the *Friendship*. They would sightsee together and enjoyed sampling the various ethnic restaurants in and around Boston. On one occasion, they took in a play, *The Good Hope*. The story was a tragic one, in which most of the characters drown. However, one of the play's recurring lines, "The fish are dearly paid for,"[3] struck the *Friendship* crew as particularly hilarious, and they adopted it as the unofficial motto for the flight, even going so far as to create a goldfish symbol to go along with it.

As the weeks wore on, Earhart also found that she and George Putnam, whom she called "G.P.," were becoming closer. What began as a business relationship had slowly blossomed into a friendship. Any attraction they felt for each other, however, was quickly cooled off. Earhart was still, at that time, seeing Sam Chapman, and Putnam was married. Nevertheless, the two continued to spend time together and grew closer as the flight drew nearer.

At long last, all the flight preparations were in order, and the *Friendship* was ready for its historic flight. The plane took off at 6:31 A.M. on June 3, 1928, flying east from Boston toward Newfoundland, Canada, the first stop on the

DID YOU KNOW?

When Amelia Earhart flew on the *Friendship*, she carried with her a copy of Richard Byrd's book *Skyward*, to be presented to Amy Phipps Guest. Inside the book, Byrd wrote the following inscription:

> I am sending you this copy of my first book by the first girl to cross the Atlantic Ocean by air—the very brave Miss Earhart. But for circumstances I well know that it would have been you who would have crossed first. I send you my heartiest congratulations and good wishes. I admire your determination and courage.[*]

[*] Amelia Earhart, *20 Hrs., 40 Min.: Our Flight in the Friendship*. Washington, D.C.: National Geographic Society, 2003, p. 50.

journey. Almost immediately after takeoff, the crew of the *Friendship* experienced its first major problem. As Earhart tried to snap a photograph of the Boston harbor below them, the spring lock on the cabin door snapped off and Earhart was forced to physically hold the door shut until Gordon, whom she called "Slim," was able to repair it. He did so by tying a gas can to the door handle, but that too began to slide, and Earhart almost slid out the door herself.

Eventually, the door was patched together by tying string to a sturdy brace inside the cabin, and the rest of the trip to Newfoundland passed without any trouble. As they flew, Earhart jotted notes in her logbook, taking in the sights around her and trying to capture the experience of air travel. Among her observations were: "I can see fifteen little fishing vessels. Probably they can't see each other. . . . I have in my ears some little rubber ear stops which Mrs. Byrd sent. She said Commander B. had used them in his transatlantic flight, and was the only one who could hear when the plane reached the other side. . . . One can see deeply into the water and mark shoals and currents. What an easy way to see what are bugaboos for surface craft. . . . The motors are humming sweetly."[4]

At last, Wilmer Stultz sailed the plane down from the clouds to a smooth landing in Halifax, Nova Scotia. The landing was unplanned, as the crew had hoped to make it all the way to Trepassey in Newfoundland. Unfortunately, bad weather and lack of visibility forced the landing in Halifax. Once they had safely touched down, however, they found they had a more urgent problem to contend with than the weather: the press. For weeks, rumors had been swirling about the flight. In particular, people were curious as to whether Earhart herself was going to be on board. Now, it seemed as though reporters were prowling about in Halifax, eager to snap a picture of the aviatrix. To avoid being detected, she remained on board the *Friendship* while Stultz and Gordon went ashore for a report on the weather. She was even forced to avoid the windows for fear that a sneaky photographer might catch her.

Eventually, Earhart was able to slip into a hotel undetected, but it did not stop the reporters from continually badgering her crewmates. At one point, things got so bad that reporters even accosted Stultz and Gordon in their room at midnight, attempting to get them to dress in their flight gear and pose for a picture. Earhart, safely hidden in the next room, could hear everything. "I am displeased with their thoughtlessness in keeping the men (Bill and Slim) awake," she said. "I don't know whether the newspaper men know I am here so I am not shouting my sentiments."[5]

IN HER OWN WORDS

This is a letter written by Amelia Earhart to her father before the flight. It was entrusted to George Putnam to be opened by Edwin Earhart in the event that his daughter's plane went down over the Atlantic.

> Dearest Dad,
>   Hooray for the last grand adventure. I wish I had won but it was worthwhile anyway. You know that.
>   I have no faith that we'll meet anywhere again, but I wish we might.
>   Anyway, goodbye, and good luck to you.
> Affectionately, your doter,
> MILL*

---

* Mary S. Lovell, *The Sound of Wings: The Life of Amelia Earhart*. New York: St. Martin's Press, 1989, p. 39.

Amelia Earhart is shown next to the *Friendship* on June 14, 1928, while in Trepassey, Newfoundland. Earhart and the other crew members of the *Friendship*—pilot Wilmer Stultz and copilot Louis Gordon— had to wait out bad weather for days in Trepassey before they could attempt their crossing of the Atlantic Ocean.

By the next morning, however, there was no concealing it any longer. The word was out, and the papers everywhere carried larger-than-life headlines trumpeting Earhart's flight across the Atlantic and referring to her as "Lady Lindy."

Waylaid by reporters at breakfast, the three fliers gave interviews and posed for pictures, but they did not have to contend with the media frenzy for long. They took off quickly from Halifax and reached Trepassey after a flight of just over four hours.

AT TREPASSEY

At that time, Trepassey was a small, isolated fishing community of only 600 people, and most of them came out to greet the crew. In fact, the children in the town's school all ran from their classes without permission to see the plane come in for a landing.

After a short stay in Trepassey, the crew hoped to be aloft early the next morning. Bad weather, however, conspired to keep them in the small fishing village for several days. During that time, Earhart familiarized herself with the townsfolk and life in this small village. The jagged rocks and shoals that surrounded Trepassey had led to a great many shipwrecks, she learned. As such, the sailors had dubbed the waters around it as "the Graveyard of the Atlantic." One woman in whose house Earhart was staying had her entire silverware collection made up of knives, forks, and spoons that had washed ashore from shipwrecks.

Finally, on June 17, after 12 days of idling in Trepassey, the weather had cleared enough for them to take off and make their way across the Atlantic. They flew through fog

IN HER OWN WORDS

Amelia Earhart reflected on the time she spent in Trepassey:

> The cruelty of country and climate is surely a contrast to the kind hearts of the people of Newfoundland. They were untiringly good to us.*

* "Out Stepped Amelia," *Newfoundland Quarterly.*
http://www.newfoundlandquarterly.ca/online435a.php.

The *Friendship* is shown flying over Burry Point, Wales, just before landing in June 1928. Amelia Earhart had become the first woman to fly across the Atlantic.

and heavy weather, with almost no visibility. Finally, after several hours of flying amid thick, rolling clouds, Stultz brought the plane down a bit so they could see where they were. Coming below the fog bank, the three fliers spotted a steamship, the *America*, plying its way across the Atlantic. Seeing the ship meant that they were not lost and were close to the shipping lanes, which was a relief to the crew. However, they still did not know where they were. Earhart tried tying a note to an orange and dropping it from the plane onto the *America's* deck. It missed by a few hundred yards, prompting her to try again. This one also missed, and they were forced to keep flying. They continued on, not knowing that the captain of the *America*, having realized who was flying above his ship, had ordered the coordinates painted on the deck.

As the flight wore on, fuel became a real worry. They had very little of it remaining, and Stultz in particular was growing concerned. Finally, just as the situation was becoming more serious, Gordon spotted land. The sight made him so excited that he accidentally threw the sandwich he was eating out the window.

Still uncertain where his plane was, Stultz brought the *Friendship* down and tied it up to a buoy. Although curious onlookers had gathered on the shore nearby, they were too far away for anyone to hear them. It was almost an hour before anyone came out to greet the fliers. When asked where they had landed, the locals informed them that the *Friendship* was moored off of Burry Point, Wales.

Amelia Earhart had done it. She had crossed the Atlantic Ocean.

Celebrity

Following their landing in Wales and the realization that their journey had been successful, the crew of the *Friendship* suddenly found everything moving very quickly. Reporters were everywhere, each wanting to hear from Amelia Earhart. Even President Calvin Coolidge had a message for her, via telegram: "TO YOU THE FIRST WOMAN SUCCESSFULLY TO SPAN THE NORTH ATLANTIC BY AIR THE GREAT ADMIRATION OF MYSELF AND THE UNITED STATES."[1]

After several hours spent in Wales, the *Friendship* took off for Southampton, England, where the media blitz continued. Earhart was the focus of the reporters' attention, but she was quick to point out the achievements of her crewmates. "I was a passenger on the journey," she told the press, "just a passenger. Everything that was done to bring us across was done by Wilmer Stultz and Slim Gordon. Any praise I can give them . . . they ought to have. You can't pile it on too thick."[2]

As noble as her sentiments were, the public still considered Earhart the true star of the *Friendship* flight. Everywhere she went, she was mobbed by well-wishers, fans, proposals of marriage. Henry Ford gave Earhart her own private limousine, and she found herself taking lunch and socializing with some of the most powerful officials in politics, including Lady Mary Heath, a fellow pilot who had made a successful solo flight from South Africa to England. Lady Heath invited Earhart to come and fly her plane, an Avro Avian. Earhart agreed and, after taking a quick trial flight, Lady Heath sold her the plane on the spot.

After a whirlwind tour of England, Earhart returned to the United States, this time by boat. Arriving in New York aboard the *President Roosevelt*, she was given a hero's welcome. Along with "Lady Lindy," the press also dubbed her "The Queen of the Air." She and the other fliers received a ticker-tape parade, followed by a ceremony during which Mayor Jimmy Walker presented her with the key to the City of New York.

AMERICAN HEROINE

From New York, Earhart traveled to Boston and then Chicago and Pittsburgh, Pennsylvania, where her reception was no less enthusiastic. Crowds lined up everywhere to see her. In Pittsburgh, she was given the chance to ride in the cab of a train, clad in engineer's cap and overalls. In Chicago, she spoke at Hyde Park High School, which she had once attended, and she shocked the audience when she left the stage by stepping off of it and onto a piano.

Following her many publicity stops, Earhart spent time at George Putnam's home in Rye, New York, working on a book chronicling the flight. The money she received from this book, after paying back Amy Phipps Guest for the cost

In July 1928, crowds in Chicago gave a warm welcome to Amelia Earhart and her *Friendship* crewmates Wilmer Stultz, left, and Louis Gordon. The press was hailing Earhart as "Lady Lindy" and "The Queen of the Air."

of the flight, finally freed her of debts. At last, after years of financial struggles, Earhart was able to help out her mother. She sent Amy Earhart letters instructing her to buy new clothes and treat herself to things that she wanted.

ACROSS THE COUNTRY

Fame and fortune, though, were secondary to what was still Earhart's first love: flying. Now, flush with success and financially stable, she set out to complete the journey she had intended to make four years earlier: a flight across the country. Using the plane she had purchased from Lady Heath, Earhart departed from New York with George Putnam in tow. Shortly into the flight, they hit their first snag. While attempting to land in a field near Pittsburgh, Earhart's plane rolled into a ditch, damaging the underside and the propeller.

Putnam immediately ordered the parts needed to repair the plane and get back under way. This was no easy feat, considering that the aircraft was English and suitable parts were hard to come by in the United States. Nevertheless, the repairs were made and Earhart was able to resume her trip.

Once again, it was not long before word got out that Earhart was attempting to fly solo across the continent, a feat that no woman had yet accomplished.

IN HER OWN WORDS

Amelia Earhart's prophetic words, written in an article for the *London Times* and the *New York Times* shortly after the flight of the *Friendship*:

> Someday women will fly the Atlantic and think little of it because it is an ordinary thing to do.*

* Susan Butler, *East to the Dawn: The Life of Amelia Earhart*. Philadelphia: Da Capo Press, 1999, p. 201.

Earhart found flying over the United States to be a trickier undertaking than perhaps she had originally thought. Looking down at the country from above, the landscape looked very similar, making it hard to differentiate one town from another. This slight dilemma later prompted her to write: "Imagine automobiling without signs! Imagine trying to recognize a new town the way fliers do—a hundred-mile-an-hour look at a checkerboard of streets and roofs, trees and fields, with highways and railroads radiating and criss-crossing, and perhaps a river or two to complicate—or simplify—the geography lesson."[3]

Complications aside, Earhart's cross-country jaunt was not without its exciting moments. During her trip, she stayed with random people she met along the way, rather than stay in hotels. She would stay with farmers and families, often putting her plane down in their back fields. On one occasion, she veered off course and had to put her plane down right in the middle of Main Street in Hobbs, New Mexico. The residents there were hospitable and gave her gasoline and a place to sleep for the night. Unfortunately, unbeknownst to her, the fuel was not good for her engine and forced a five-day stopover in Pecos, Texas, for repairs.

Finally, Earhart reached California in time for the National Air Races, where she received a standing ovation from those in attendance. After a brief stay in the Golden State, during which she visited with her father, Earhart returned to New York. After a slight layover in Utah for repairs, she arrived in New York on October 16, 1928, and was hailed as the first woman ever to make a solo-return transcontinental flight.

ENDORSEMENTS

Upon her return to New York, Earhart's celebrity image continued to grow. She endorsed a variety of products, from luggage to women's clothing. A cigarette company, Lucky

Strike, also asked for her endorsement, which she initially refused, as she did not smoke. It was pointed out, however, that her *Friendship* crewmates Wilmer Stultz and Louis Gordon *did* smoke (which was considered fashionable at the time, given the world's ignorance of the damaging effects of cigarettes), and she agreed.

Around this time, Earhart was also made an associate editor at *Cosmopolitan* magazine, a trendy periodical that published fiction and articles on fashion and topical events. In publication since 1886, it is still in existence today. Her job at the magazine was to provide eight articles a year on the subject of aviation, and she used the forum as a place to campaign for a greater role for women in aviation.

In fact, Earhart's campaigning for aviation was not limited to her feelings on gender. She was a staunch supporter of air travel overall and was determined to help open the world's eyes to the idea. In the late 1920s, flying was still very much a novelty and not something the average person did. The idea of getting in a plane and flying across the country, the ocean, or just about anywhere seemed unthinkable to the people of this time, and Earhart sought to change their minds. She teamed up with aviation magnates Jack Maddux and C.M. Keys, cofounders of Transcontinental Air Transport, to help promote air travel from a female perspective. Also helping to promote TAT was Charles Lindbergh, who created a cross-country route, dubbed the "Lindbergh Line," in which passengers flew during the day and then slept at night in Pullman train cars.

In July 1929, Earhart was on hand at New York's Penn Station to christen one of TAT's airplanes, *The City of New York*. She also wrote one of her eight articles for *Cosmopolitan* about TAT and the rise of passenger airlines. Unfortunately, her timing could not have been more off. Shortly after the article ran, one of TAT's planes, *The City of San Francisco*, crashed into a mountainside outside of

Albuquerque, New Mexico, with no survivors. Not long after that, there was another crash, this time in California, again with no survivors.

"THE POWDER PUFF AIR DERBY"

Nevertheless, Earhart soldiered on. She continued to fly, of course, upgrading her Avian plane for a five-passenger Vega and participating in the Women's Air Derby, an air race that would take female fliers from Santa Monica, California, to Cleveland, Ohio. Derisively named "The Powder Puff Air Derby," the air race was seen by some as a disaster waiting to happen. Few people trusted women in the air, and most foresaw the race ending in tragedy.

So serious were some people's concerns that the ideas were broached of having a male navigator accompany the women and moving the race east of the Rocky Mountains to avoid a calamity.

These hurdles aside, 19 female pilots took off from Clover Field in Santa Monica on August 18. One pilot, Mary von Mach, turned back almost immediately. She eventually got back in the air and finished the race, but her actions led to her disqualification. For the rest of the female pilots, the race was a grueling test of their resolve and skill as pilots. They flew from checkpoint to checkpoint, stopping to rest and refuel and then taking to the air again at dawn.

Danger was everywhere, and misfortune was in the air, quite literally. One pilot, Marvel Crosson, lost her life when her engine failed and her parachute refused to open. Another woman, Margaret Perry, was struck with typhoid fever and placed in a Texas hospital. Blanche Noyes's plane caught on fire, while Bobbi Trout crashed her plane somewhere in Mexico, walking away from the wreckage alive but out of the race.

By the end of the race, the women had traveled nearly 2,500 miles (4,000 kilometers) and been on the move for nine days. When they arrived in Columbus, Ohio, the last stopover before the finish line in Cleveland, 20,000 people had come out to meet them.

The race was won by Louise Thaden, who took home $3,600. Earhart came in third and won $875, but winning the race had never been of primary importance to her. For her, the Women's Air Derby was a chance to prove that female fliers were neither a novelty nor an aberration. They were a vital part of the aviation landscape, and they were here to stay.

To further drive her point home, Earhart began to put together a group of female pilots. The purpose of the group was to establish equality for women in aviation, keep female pilots in communication with each other, and ensure better winnings for women pilots in aerial competition. A letter from Neva Paris, Fay Gillis, Margorie Brown, and Frances Harrell was sent out to the more than 120 licensed female pilots in the United States. Of those, 99 replied. Thus the Ninety-Nines were born, and Earhart was elected the organization's first president. More than 80 years later, the Ninety-Nines are still in existence and still ensure fair and equal treatment for women pilots all over the world.

LOVE AND MARRIAGE

Amid all the excitement following her flight across the Atlantic, something unexpected was happening to Amelia Earhart. She was falling in love with George Putnam.

Since first signing her up for the flight of the *Friendship*, Putnam had never been far from her side, nor she from his. She wrote her book *20 Hrs., 40 Min.* at Putnam's home in Rye, brought him with her on the first leg of her cross-country flight, and when she landed in Cleveland at the end of the Women's Air Derby, Putnam was the one who was there to greet her.

Putnam had divorced his first wife, Dorothy Binney, in December 1929. There was no bitterness between the two, and less than a month later, Dorothy married Frank Upton, a steamship captain. The divorce left Putnam free to pursue Earhart, which he did with a vengeance. Earhart, though, was uncertain. As her relationship to Sam Chapman proved, she was not interested in being tied down. Nevertheless, Putnam proved persuasive, and Earhart could not deny her feelings. On February 7, 1931, in a small and simple ceremony at a Putnam relative's house, Amelia Earhart and George Putnam became husband and wife.

Agreeing to marry Putnam, in Earhart's eyes, did not mean that she was giving up her flying career or changing who she was to become a timid housewife. To drive this point home, probably to herself as much as Putnam, she composed him a letter, detailing how she felt about their arrangement. In it, she wrote:

> In our life together, I shall not hold you to any medieval code of faithfulness to me, nor shall I consider myself bound to you similarly. If we can be honest I think the difficulties which arise may be best avoided. . . .
>
> Please let us not interfere with the other's work or play, nor let the world see our private joys or disagreements. In this connection I may have to keep some place where I can go to be myself now and then, for I cannot guarantee to endure at all the confinements of even an attractive cage.[4]

At the end of the letter, she asked Putnam to promise to let her go if they were not happy within a year of being married.

After her transatlantic journey in 1928, Amelia Earhart and George Palmer Putnam grew close. Less than three years later, in February 1931, the two were married. Earhart made it clear that she was not going to give up her career now that she was married.

The letter did not seem to trouble Putnam much. He kept it with him and did not reveal it to the public until long after Earhart's disappearance. Whatever his thoughts were about what Earhart wrote, the ceremony went on as planned and the two were married.

They did not take time for a honeymoon, however. True to her letter, Earhart was not about to let marriage keep her from doing what she was born to do. By 1931, she had flown solo across America three times. Now she had her sights set on the Atlantic Ocean, the next great challenge awaiting women pilots.

Flying
the Atlantic

Immediately following her marriage, Amelia Earhart wasted no time in attempting to shatter more flight records. The only issue was, there were fewer and fewer records to break. With more and more women pilots out there setting their own records, the pie was growing smaller and smaller. Nevertheless, Earhart searched the aviation landscape and finally came upon what seemed to be the next big thing: the autogiro.

A bizarre mixture of an airplane and a helicopter, the autogiro was purchased by George Putnam from its manufacturer, a company called Pitcairn. In April 1931, Earhart set an altitude record in the unusual craft, reaching an unofficial height of 19,000 feet (5,800 meters) on one flight and an official height of 18,451 feet (5,624 meters) on another.

With these records in place, there was only one logical step: to take the autogiro across the country. With Putnam's help, they secured sponsorship from the Beech-Nut chewing gum company, and, on May 29, Earhart and mechanic Eddie Gorski took off from Newark, New Jersey, and landed in Oakland, California, on June 6 (although some reports have her landing on June 7). Unfortunately, she discovered upon landing that the honor of making the first-ever cross-country autogiro flight was not hers. Johnny Miller, a 25-year-old professional pilot from Poughkeepsie, New York, had beaten her to the coast by a week. Earhart was disappointed but did not let the defeat get her down. She returned to New York and continued to champion the autogiro, even going so far as to write an article for *Cosmopolitan* titled, "Your Next Garage May House an Autogiro," in which she envisioned a future in which average people commuted to and from work in these unique flying machines.

Earhart spent much of the rest of 1931 demonstrating the autogiro around the country. It did not always go smoothly. On one occasion, during her flight home from California, she crashed the craft when its rotors clipped a landing light on takeoff in Abilene, Texas. The autogiro came down in a nearby parking lot, damaging some of the cars and spraying the crowd with shards of debris. Thankfully, no one was injured, Earhart included, and a replacement autogiro was sent to her immediately.

A few months later, at an air show in Detroit, there was another crash. Putnam was present at this one and remembered seeing the downed aircraft:

> As I swung round I saw the giro, its rotors splintered, disappear in a cloud of smoke. I vaulted the rail and raced for the wreck. Never have I run so

George Putnam lent Amelia Earhart a hand as she climbed out of the cockpit of her autogiro after completing a transcontinental flight to the West Coast and back. The autogiro was an odd combination of airplane and helicopter.

fast, until one of those guy wires caught my pumping legs exactly at the ankles. I did a complete outside loop, up into the air and over, landing full on my back. . . . Coming to my senses—some of them at least—I saw AE emerge from the welter of dust (it wasn't smoke) and wave her hands in the air to show she was unhurt.[1]

Again, Earhart escaped the crash without injury, but it was clear her enthusiasm for the autogiro was waning. It was time for her to focus on something new.

Around this time, as she was working on her second book, Earhart became interested in the prospect of flying the Atlantic solo. She was eager for a new challenge, as well as the chance to prove to people that her fame and success were due to more than her being a passenger on a famous flight. She wanted to make her mark on her own, and a solo Atlantic crossing was the way to do that.

No one had crossed the ocean by air to Europe alone since Charles Lindbergh, so Earhart had to ensure that her flight was well prepared. With that notion in mind, she contacted Norwegian pilot Bernt Balchen. Balchen was famous for flying the *America* on Commander Richard Byrd's South Pole expedition and traveling with Roald Amundsen to the North Pole via dirigible. He was efficient and thorough in his preparations, going over Earhart's plane rivet by rivet and making modifications where he saw fit. He and mechanic Eddie Gorski strengthened the fuselage by running braces along it. They also added more space for fuel tanks to ensure that Earhart had enough to make the journey across the ocean. When they were done, the plane could hold 420 gallons (1,590 liters) of gas, allowing it to travel approximately 3,200 miles (5,150 kilometers).

Secrecy was a large part of the operation, much as it was when the *Friendship* flight was being planned. As far as the public knew, the Vega was being retrofitted in preparation for a possible flight to the South Pole involving Balchen and Lincoln Ellsworth.

Balchen's efficiency and attention to detail took a great deal of pressure off Earhart. With Balchen in charge of the retrofit, she was free to concentrate on other preparations for the flight, such as learning how to "fly blind." Portions of her route over the great expanse of the Atlantic would take her through patches of fog and, given the length of the journey, flying in darkness was also inevitable. As a result, Earhart spent countless hours mastering instrumentation, learning about the weather, and studying maps.

Finally, on the morning of May 20, 1932, Earhart traveled to Teterboro airport in New Jersey to assess the flying conditions. In the early afternoon, she received a phone call from Putnam. He had spent the morning going over weather bulletins from Atlantic shipping and was reporting clear skies all the way to Newfoundland. After a quick conversation with Balchen, Earhart agreed that it was now or never. She raced back home to Rye, New York, to grab her flying gear, along with some maps and charts, a comb, a toothbrush, and a thermos. She also took a few moments to enjoy the peacefulness of her home before undertaking this dangerous journey. "Five minutes was enough to pick up my things," she recalled. "Plus a lingering few more to drink in the beauty of a treasured sight. Beside and below our bedroom windows were dogwood trees, their blossoms in luxuriant full flower, unbelievable bouquets of white and pink flecked with the sunshine of spring."[2] Her things packed, her thoughts collected, Earhart left her home in Rye and returned to New Jersey. Less than a half hour after returning to Teterboro, Amelia Earhart was airborne.

On the flight to Harbor Grace, Newfoundland, Earhart and Gorski rested in the cabin behind the fuel tank while Balchen manned the controls. Once they landed, Earhart went to take a nap to be well rested for her flight while Gorski and Balchen made a few final preparations. Around 6:30 P.M., she woke up and headed out to the field. Writing in his diary, Balchen painted this picture of the aviatrix just before her flight:

> She listens calmly, only biting her lip a little, as I go over with her the course to hold, and tell her what weather she can expect on the way across the ocean. She looks at me with a small lonely smile and says, "Do you think I can make it?" and I grin back: "You bet." She crawls calmly into the cockpit of the big empty airplane, starts the engine, runs it up, checks the mags, and nods her head. We pull the chocks and she is off.[3]

ALONE OVER THE ATLANTIC

Earhart's first solo Atlantic flight went smoothly for the first few hours. The skies were clear as she made her way east, looking down at icebergs and boats floating on the water. But as she cruised gently over the moonlit ocean, Earhart's altimeter suddenly gave out. Now she had no way of gauging how high over the water she was—a potentially disastrous situation. Luckily, she also had a barograph on board and was able to at least glean a rough idea of how high she was.

Unfortunately, the failure of the altimeter was not the only hitch in Earhart's transatlantic journey. As she flew, the plane's exhaust manifold began to separate, the result of a bad weld. The separation caused the plane to vibrate, and looking over the instrument panel, Earhart noticed a small blue flame burning through the break. The flames were not a major cause for concern, being the result of the fuel and air meeting under pressure, but the split was nevertheless troublesome.

Earhart, however, decided it made more sense to soldier on rather than try to turn back to Harbor Grace.

As her flight continued, a lightning storm rose up and slammed her plane, buffeting it this way and that. The black storm clouds were too high to fly over, and Earhart had no choice but to plow her way through them. At one point, ice began to form on the plane, freezing the controls and sending it into a spin, as she later recalled: "I do know that I tried my best to do exactly what one should do with a spinning plane, and regained flying control as the warmth of the lower altitude melted the ice. As we righted and held level again, through the blackness below I could see the whitecaps, too close for comfort."[4]

As morning came, Earhart had, after a rough night of flying, reached a comfortable altitude of about 10,000 feet (3,048 meters). Her problems, however, had not gone away. The shaking had increased, suggesting that the problem with the manifold had gotten worse.

At last her worries came to an end when Earhart spotted land. Out of her window, the green hills of Ireland could be seen on the horizon. Recalling the moment, she later wrote:

Probably more exciting than actually sighting land was seeing a small fishing vessel about 100 miles [161 kilometers] off the coast. I was going by, as I wanted to reach land, but then decided to circle, that all might know I had got so far, anyway. I circled and received an answering signal. A whistle and some kind of bomb was sent off. Of course I could not hear them, but I could see the smoke and the steam from the whistle. It was the first human contact since Newfoundland.[5]

Without an altimeter, Earhart had no real way of determining precisely where she was. As a result, she used a trick she learned while flying across the United States and relied on the landscape below to orient her. Following a railroad track along the ground, Earhart eventually came down in a pasture amid a herd of grazing cows, much to the bemusement of the Irish farmer who watched her land.

Despite her odd choice of landing sites, Earhart had plenty to celebrate. Not only was she now officially the first woman to fly solo across the Atlantic, she was also the first person of either sex to ever fly the Atlantic twice. On top of that, she had also set a world record for crossing the Atlantic in the shortest time (14 hours, 54 minutes) and set another record for the longest distance ever flown nonstop by a woman (2,026 miles, or 3,261 kilometers).

Nevertheless, Earhart was disappointed, as she had hoped to fly all the way to France, as Charles Lindbergh had done. In her first statement, she acknowledged this shortcoming by saying, "Tell my friends in New York I am very glad to have come across successfully, but I am sorry I didn't make France."[6] Most people were simply elated that she had survived the flight at all and realized that, France or not, she had successfully achieved her goal. Some, though, took the opportunity to sneer at Earhart's perceived missing of the mark. The *New York Post* published a scathing write-up titled "About All She Has Proved," which blasted both Earhart and the overall flight. "We think it an almost entirely silly and useless performance," the paper observed. "About all she has proved is that well-known phenomenon of nature that a girl can't jump quite as far as a boy can."[7]

The *Post*'s barbs aside, the rest of the world joined Earhart in celebration. After spending the night at the thatched cottage of the farmer whose field she landed in, Earhart traveled to Londonderry, Ireland, where, at the Associated Press office, telegrams and cables from fans were pouring in from all over the globe. Earhart received letters from the president of the United States, the prime minister of Britain, and Charles Lindbergh himself.

From Ireland, Earhart embarked on a whirlwind tour of Europe, beginning in London, where she stayed at the American Embassy as a guest of the ambassador. She had to borrow clothes from the ambassador's wife, as she had only the clothes she was wearing when she left Teterboro.

HONORS AND AWARDS

Throughout Europe, Earhart was showered with praise and a host of awards. In England, she received an honorary membership in the British Guild of Airpilots and Navigators and so enchanted the Prince of Wales during their visit that he extended the meeting by 15 minutes, leading some to speculate (incorrectly) that a romance was blooming between the two.

From London, she was off to Paris on the *Evadne*, the yacht of aircraft manufacturer C.R. Fairey. Here she met up with her husband at last. The two of them celebrated Earhart's success with more accolades and audiences. She laid a wreath on the Tomb of the Unknown Soldier and was given the Cross of the Knight of the Legion of Honor by Paul Painlevé, the French minister of air, who had awarded the same medal to Charles Lindbergh five years earlier.

In the days following Earhart's arrival, Paris was alive with the rich and famous summering in the city, all of whom were happy to host Earhart and Putnam. They also were showered with adulation from the public. Everywhere she went, Earhart shook hands with people and posed for pictures. Flowers came in by the truckload, filling their hotel room from floor to ceiling (which wreaked havoc on Putnam's hay fever).

On June 15, Earhart's European tour came to an end. She and Putnam departed for the United States aboard the ocean liner *Ile de France* amid the cheers of a crowd that

Thousands assembled at City Hall in New York City to welcome Amelia Earhart after her solo transatlantic flight in 1932. Later, in Washington, D.C., Earhart received a gold medal from the National Geographic Society.

had gathered on the dock to see her off. Much to Earhart's delight, three light airplanes flew overhead and dropped flowers onto the deck in a gesture of farewell. It was a fitting end to Earhart's journey through Europe and a symbol of just how much of a star she had become.

Back in America, the adulation continued. Earhart received a ticker-tape parade in New York City, attended by thousands of people who cheered her on as she passed.

In Washington, D.C., Earhart was awarded the gold medal from the National Geographic Society, the same medal that Lindbergh received five years earlier. Earhart was the first woman to receive the medal, and the ceremony was attended by the president, the chief justice of the Supreme Court, the secretaries of state, treasury and commerce, the attorney general, high-ranking members of three branches of the military, and diplomats representing 22 nations.

In the wake of her astounding success, one might think that Earhart would simply bask in its glow and reap the rewards. Instead, she set her sights on breaking more records. Specifically, she wanted to become the first woman to fly nonstop across America. With Putnam's new appointment to the editorial board of Paramount Pictures in Los Angeles,

NIGHT FLIGHT WITH THE FIRST LADY

Amelia Earhart's celebrity status made her a frequent guest at the White House, and she and George Putnam became good friends with President Franklin Delano Roosevelt and his wife, Eleanor. During one visit in April 1933, the first lady confided to Earhart that she had never flown at night. Without hesitation, Earhart contacted Eastern Airlines and made arrangements for a quick flight. Still dressed in their evening wear, the women went out to the airfield and up into the Washington night. Once airborne, Earhart turned out the cabin lights, allowing Mrs. Roosevelt to see the lights of the city fully. Earhart even turned the controls over to the first lady for a while. When they landed, the women were so thrilled they kept the excitement going by borrowing Mrs. Roosevelt's brother's car and taking it for a drive.

she had her chance. She and Putnam flew to Los Angeles on July 1 and attended the 1932 Summer Olympic Games. Less than 10 days later, she departed California en route to Newark, New Jersey. Unfortunately, a stopover in Columbus, Ohio, for a fuel line repair put an end to her hopes of a non-stop flight. Earhart did manage to break a record nevertheless. With a flying time of 19 hours, 14 minutes, and 40 seconds, she eclipsed the record for a coast-to-coast flight by a female pilot. The previous record holder, Ruth Nichols, managed the flight in 29 hours, 1 minute, and 49 seconds. Earhart had broken the record by nearly 10 hours.

A few weeks later, she returned to California and made a second grab at the record. This time she touched down in New Jersey after 19 hours, 7 minutes, and 56 seconds in the air. With that, it was official. Amelia Earhart was the first woman to fly nonstop across America.

With two astounding successes in one year, Earhart had dispelled the notion that the *Friendship* flight was a fluke. She had proved that she was an aviator on par with the best of them. Now the question was, what would she do next?

To the
Pacific

The Bendix Air Race was considered the premier aviation event in America. Some even compared it to the
Kentucky Derby. So when the 1933 Bendix Race started
on July 1, Amelia Earhart was there to participate. She and
Ruth Nichols were the only two female fliers in attendance.
This was the first year that women were allowed to participate in the cross-country air race, and Earhart was eager
to be involved. She and Nichols were in competition for a
prize of $2,500.

Earhart left New York on July 1 and was doing well
until, somewhere over Wichita, Kansas, her engine over-
heated, forcing her down. After an overnight stay in the
Sunflower State, Earhart was back in the air, only to have
the hatch cover blow open. She flew more than 70 miles

Amelia Earhart and Ruth Nichols were the first two women to compete in the Bendix Air Race, the nation's premier flying competition. Earhart finished the 1933 cross-country race ahead of Nichols, earning a $2,500 first-place prize and a $2,000 bonus.

(113 kilometers) holding it down with her hand before landing in Arizona to have it repaired. Nevertheless, she managed to land in Los Angeles ahead of Nichols. She received a $2,000 bonus for being the first woman ever to finish the Bendix Air Race.

THE CALL OF THE PACIFIC

In the summer of 1934, Earhart and George Putnam took a break from the maelstrom of their lives for a much-needed vacation in the mountains of Wyoming. Afterward, they spent much of their time on the West Coast as Putnam settled into his new role at Paramount Pictures. The time in California planted an idea in Earhart's mind. She wanted to fly 2,500 miles (4,000 kilometers) from Hawaii to California. One evening, as Putnam was coming home from work, she sprung this news on him. He recalled: "One night in the autumn of 1934 she sat in golden crepe pyjamas . . . at Rye reading the evening paper. As I came in from the train, she looked up in the way of a person thinking out loud and said, 'I want to fly the Pacific soon.'"[1]

At the Lockheed factory in Burbank, California, Earhart's plane was overhauled in preparation for the flight. Overseeing the job was Paul Mantz, a former army pilot Putnam had met while working on *Wings*, a 1927 movie for Paramount Pictures that was the first film to win the Academy Award for Best Picture. A skilled pilot and keen-eyed technician, Mantz was a perfect choice to help get Earhart's plane ready for its flight.

TRAGEDY

As Amelia Earhart was in California, beginning the preparations for her Pacific flight, George Putnam telephoned from New York with the devastating news that a significant portion of their home in Rye had been destroyed in a fire. Many valuable and irreplaceable items were lost, including a trunk containing Earhart's writings and poetry going all the way back to her childhood.

On December 22, 1934, Earhart and Putnam, along with Mantz and his wife, Myrtle, set sail for Hawaii aboard the ocean liner SS *Lurline*. Speculation was rampant that the aviatrix was going to make a go at a transpacific flight, but she denied it vehemently. Upon her arrival in Honolulu, reporters swamped Earhart, pressing the issue. Her answers were reserved, telling people that she merely intended to do some flying around the Hawaiian islands. Few people were buying it, however.

As speculation from the outside world mounted, Earhart and her crew went to work preparing to make the flight. They set up shop at a beachfront home in Waikiki, where they remained for the holidays. Meanwhile, at nearby Wheeler Field, a team of army engineers was going over her plane rivet by rivet to ensure its readiness for the journey.

As detailed as their preparations were, the flight was nearly grounded before it even reached the tarmac. Almost from the beginning, the papers condemned Earhart for daring to cross the Pacific on her own. The risks, they claimed, were too great. Ten pilots had already been lost making the flight, and there was concern that Earhart would certainly join their ranks. Her plane was too small, they argued, and should she be lost, it would result in a costly search that could put more pilots in danger.

Compounding the problem, the navy suddenly decided not to clear Earhart for departure, saying her radio did not have the necessary range to transmit the 2,500-mile (4,000-kilometer) distance from Hawaii to Los Angeles. This hurdle was overcome when Mantz took the plane up to 12,000 feet (3,658 meters) and was able to reach Kingman, Arizona, without issue. Without a leg to stand on, the navy dropped the argument and cleared Earhart to fly.

The final hurdle in the storm of controversy surrounding Earhart's gamble for the Pacific was a dustup with the Hawaiian businessmen who had put up $10,000 to sponsor

the flight. The businessmen, mostly pineapple and sug-
arcane growers, became the target of accusations that the
money was part of a campaign to buy favorable taxes on
U.S. sales of Hawaiian sugar. Nervous that, should Earhart
be lost, the bad publicity could seriously harm their businesses, the men tried to back out of the deal. Fuming,
Earhart stormed into a meeting at the luxurious Royal
Hawaiian Hotel dressed in her leather jacket and jodhpurs
and faced the men directly. Confronted with her anger, they
backed down and agreed to support the flight.

On January 11, 1935, everything fell into place. The
weather was right, the business concerns had been ironed
out, and the world was ready to see if Amelia Earhart could
make history again.

A heavy rain that morning had dried up by about four
in the afternoon, and Earhart and Putnam traveled to

IN HER OWN WORDS

When some Hawaiian businessmen decided to renege on their
offer of $10,000 to support her Pacific flight, Amelia Earhart
confronted them, saying:

> Gentlemen, there is an aroma of cowardice in this air. You
> know as well as I do that the rumor is trash, but if you
> can be intimidated, it might as well be true. Whether you
> live in fear or defend your integrity is your decision. I have
> made mine. I intend to fly to California within this next
> week, with or without your support.*

* Susan Butler, East to the Dawn: The Life of Amelia Earhart.
Philadelphia: Da Capo Press, 1999, p. 325.

Wheeler Field to make preparations for the flight. Earhart's Vega was loaded up with 500 gallons (1,893 liters) of fuel. That weight, combined with all the equipment she carried onboard, made many people nervous that Earhart's flight might not even get off the ground. Both Mantz and Earhart felt that the plane would need 3,000 feet (914 meters) to take off. The runway at Wheeler Field was 6,000 feet (1,829 meters), twice the length, and therefore presented no problem. Still, as she brought the nose up and took off on her historic flight, Earhart flew over a group of fire trucks and military personnel carrying fire extinguishers, all ready in case something went wrong. Passing overhead, she could see the anxiety in their faces.

SMOOTH FLYING

While some of her previous flights had been marked by occasional bouts of loneliness, periods of isolation, mechanical problems, and pockets of bad weather, Earhart's Pacific journey was quite pleasant. For one thing, she had plenty of company. All the ships traveling between Hawaii and the mainland were scanning the skies for her, searchlights blazing. If any of them spotted her, they quickly radioed her position. At one point over the ocean, she was able to receive a Morse code transmission from a ship, informing her that she was on course.

Her onboard radio was a lifesaver as well. Although she did not enjoy the process of having to unreel the long antenna through a hole in the cabin floor, the radio did allow her to keep in constant contact with the mainland and listen to broadcasts from local radio stations. She was even able to speak with her husband via a radio station broadcasting out of Honolulu. With this conversation, Earhart and Putnam achieved another first, the first two-way radio contact on a civilian flight.

Scores of people surrounded Amelia Earhart's Lockheed Vega at Oakland Airport after she completed her January 1935 flight from Hawaii to California. Unlike many of her previous long-distance flights, Earhart's trip across the Pacific was smooth and uneventful.

Eighteen hours after leaving Honolulu, Earhart fell in line behind the *President Pierce*, flying in its wake en route to San Francisco. Seeing the ship let her know that she was on target. Flying low over the coast, Earhart shot over San Francisco Bay, radioed that she was on course and coming in for a landing, and set down at Oakland Airport. Officially, she was now the first person ever to fly solo across the Pacific, as well as the first person to fly solo across both the Atlantic and Pacific oceans.

A crowd of thousands had gathered to welcome Earhart to California, but at first they did not even see her, for she had landed on the far end of the runway. Once they spotted her, though, there was no containing their elation, or the world's. Reporters clamored for a quote from her, policemen held back crowds, a letter arrived from the president extending his congratulations. In the papers, the generally reserved *New York Times* praised Earhart, writing, "She now holds the fair planet in her hands."[2]

MEXICAN ODYSSEY

Not long after making history over the Pacific, Earhart was invited on a goodwill visit to Mexico by Mexican consul general Eduardo Villaseñor. While the opportunity for a historic flight was not present, as Charles Lindbergh had already flown from Washington, D.C., to Mexico City in 1927, Earhart still felt that the trip presented some interesting possibilities. For one thing, she observed, she would be the first person to fly from California to Mexico. In addition, she would also be the first person to fly from Mexico City to Newark, New Jersey.

On April 19, Earhart prepared to take off. Before she could become airborne, however, it was discovered that

IN HER OWN WORDS

Recalling the more romantic details of her flight across the Pacific, Amelia Earhart said:

> It was a night of stars. Of tropic loveliness. Stars hung outside my cockpit window near enough to touch.*

* Susan Butler, *East to the Dawn: The Life of Amelia Earhart.* Philadelphia: Da Capo Press, 1999, p. 327.

an unknown saboteur had placed a drop of acid on the rudder cables. The cables had almost been eaten through entirely. With this problem rectified, Earhart got under way just before midnight, bound for Mexico. During the flight, she lost her way and ended up being forced to land in a dry lakebed some 50 miles (80 kilometers) south of Mexico City. A band of peasants from the small village of Nopala helped Earhart get back on course, and she arrived at Valbuena Airport in just over 13½ hours.

President Lázaro Cárdenas welcomed Earhart as an honored guest, and a great many celebrations were held during her time in Mexico. During her extended 18-day stay—a result of unfavorable weather conditions—Earhart was whisked from one event to the next, allowing her little time to delve into any of the humanitarian work she had hoped to accomplish on the trip, such as meeting with some of the working women of Mexico.

Eventually, on May 8, Earhart was able to take off for her return trip to America. Preparations for the flight were great, as the higher elevation of Mexico City resulted in a thinner atmosphere, meaning takeoff in the fully loaded Vega would be more difficult than it would be at sea level. Immediately, Colonel Roberto Fierro, the chief of Mexican Military Aviation, put a team of soldiers to work fashioning a custom-built, three-mile-long (five-kilometer-long) runway in the dried-out bed of Lake Texcoco. After their work was completed, the soldiers remained behind to guard Earhart's plane and keep the area clear of everything from onlookers to cows, goats, and horses.

Early in the morning on May 8, Earhart was bade farewell by Mexican officials, including Samuel Rojas, commander of the First Air Regiment. When she finally got under way, Earhart found that her plane needed almost the entire length of the runway to generate enough speed to leave the ground. Recalling leaving Mexico, Earhart later said:

> Slowly I climbed to 10,000 feet [3,048 meters], to skim over the mountains that hem in the high central valley where the city lies, separating it from the lands that slope down to the sea. Majestic Popocatepetl raised its snowy head to the south, luminous in the rays of the rising sun. A fairyland of beauty lay below and about me—so lovely as almost to distract a pilot's attention from the task at hand, that of herding a heavy plane out of that great upland saucer and over the mountains that make its rim.[3]

Earhart returned to the United States, landing in Newark, New Jersey. A line of cars stretched out into the night at the airport, all of them waiting to see Earhart make her landing. Some reports had as many as 15,000 people gathered to witness her return.

At last, she touched down with an official flight time of 14 hours and 18 minutes. A decade earlier, Charles Lindbergh had flown from Mexico City to Washington, D.C., in 27 hours, a record Earhart easily surpassed. In total, she set three records: the nonstop intercity record between Mexico City and Newark, a new women's speed record for the 2,100 miles (3,380 kilometers) she traveled, and a new record for flying from Mexico to Washington, D.C., in which she beat Lindbergh's time by 14 hours.

Earhart was now not just a great female pilot. With her latest feat, she was officially one of the greatest fliers of all time, man or woman. She had shattered records, defied expectations, pushed boundaries, and rewritten the rules of aviation. But all of this was merely a preamble to what she knew would be her greatest achievement.

ENTERING ACADEMIA

Besides her role as the premier aviator in the world, Earhart had also become an in-demand speaker. She traveled around the country, lecturing to some 80,000 people in total and collecting $300 per appearance. To further stretch her reach beyond the world of flying, in 1935, Earhart accepted a position at Purdue University as a lecturer and consultant in the department for the study of careers for women, with a salary of $2,000 a year.

Of course, the job also came with some excellent benefits. Purdue was outfitted with a top-notch aeronautics department and, even better, its own airfield. At the university, Earhart realized, she could not only use her influence in the lecture hall, but she could also use it, and the school's resources, to conduct further research in the field of aviation. The university president, Dr. Edward Elliott, agreed with Earhart and reached out to his circle of friends and peers in search of donations to go toward funding this research. He hosted a dinner party in the fall of 1935, at which Earhart laid out her plans for a "flying laboratory." That very night, a guest of Elliott's named David Ross donated $50,000 toward the project, with an additional $30,000 coming from various benefactors including the Goodrich and Goodyear companies.

Flush with $80,000 in donations, Earhart founded the "Amelia Earhart Fund for Aeronautical Research," with the money going toward the purchase of an Electra, a two-motored plane generally regarded as the fastest in the world, with a speed of up to 210 miles per hour (338 kilometers per hour). It was also capable of reaching an altitude of 27,000 feet (8,230 meters). At the time, Earhart and millionaire aviation guru Howard Hughes were the only two people to actually own one.

For Earhart, however, owning the Electra represented more than just achievement, success, or even scientific research. To her it was a means to an end. Almost immediately after taking delivery, she had the plane outfitted and prepped for a flight that would take it almost 4,500 miles (7,250 kilometers).

Amelia Earhart had conquered the land, sea, and sky. Now there was only one thing left to do. She was going to fly around the world.

Around
the World

Although a flight around the world had already been achieved (by a U.S. Army air service team in 1924, by explorer Wolfgang von Gronau in 1932, and twice by famed aviator Wiley Post in 1931 and 1933), Amelia Earhart knew there was still great value in such an undertaking. Aside from being the first woman to attempt the journey, Earhart planned to travel along the equator, the imaginary line that circled the globe at its midpoint, in order to log the longest possible distance.

By 1936, the world had begun to grow weary of aviation firsts. It seemed that all the major records had been set or broken several times over. Earhart realized that this flight had to have more than just sensationalism going for it. She also felt that there was much to be gained scientifically from the trip, and she hoped to make great strides in aviation by reporting on how the Electra's equipment performed under such challenging conditions.

Now that her mind had been made up, Earhart set about the task of preparing to fly around the world. The first major step was plotting out a route. The decision to fly along the equator presented some significant challenges. The previous trans-global flights had avoided having to cross the expanse of the Pacific by traveling north through Alaska. For Earhart's journey, such a shortcut could not be taken. As a result, refueling the plane was an issue. Luckily, the Department of Commerce had recently claimed a number of Pacific islands. One of these was Howland Island, a small, uninhabited speck of land in the middle of the ocean. An airfield had been constructed in preparation for flights to Australia. It was the perfect spot for Earhart to refuel on the Pacific leg of her flight.

FLIGHT PLAN

Earhart's flight around the world began to come together. She now had a planned route that would begin in Oakland and then on to Honolulu. From there, she would travel to the refueling point on Howland Island and then to Australia. She would then fly to Saudi Arabia (then known just as Arabia), passing over India. From Arabia it was on to Africa, then a flight across the South Atlantic to Brazil. The final legs of the flight would carry her from Brazil to New York and then back to Oakland.

Arranging for this trip meant cutting through a mountain of red tape. Every country had its own rules and regulations for air travel and landings. Earhart needed all the proper traveling papers such as passports and visas, as well as immunizations against local diseases and permissions to fly in foreign airspace. With help from the Roosevelts,

Earhart was able to navigate the labyrinth of requests, forms, and paperwork with little difficulty.

There were also technical issues to iron out. Of paramount importance was the radio equipment. A functioning, top-level radio had been a vital component of the Pacific flight, and Earhart wanted to make sure she had the best equipment available. She did not want to have to resort to using a telegraph, as she had enjoyed the use of the radio and was out of practice in her telegraphy, having most likely not used it since crossing the Atlantic nearly five years earlier.

In the end, Western Electric came through for Earhart, supplying her with a 50-watt transmitter and an adjustable four-band receiver. The receiver could transmit on standard aircraft frequencies but had also been modified to broadcast on an emergency frequency, which could be used in conjunction with a code-transmitting key. Using the emergency frequency required a 250-foot (76-meter) trailing aerial. This aerial had to be reeled in and out using a handle and could be unreliable. Since the wire ended in a heavy leaden ball, it could snap under the strain of flying through the air at full speed, rendering it useless. Nevertheless, Earhart was glad to have the radio on board, knowing that it would be a valuable tool to have in an emergency.

When all the plans had been sketched out, Earhart officially announced her intention to become the first woman to fly around the world. The announcement was made on February 12, 1937, at the Barclay Hotel in New York City. In attendance was Henry Manning, the man Earhart had chosen to serve as her navigator. Manning was a pilot and a ship's captain. He and Earhart had met when she was returning home from England after the *Friendship* flight. Manning had been captain of the *President Roosevelt*, the ship that had brought her to America, and the two had discussed undertaking a project together. Using a globe to illustrate her flight plan, Earhart told the battery of reporters that the around-the-world flight would cover approximately 27,000 miles (43,450 kilometers).

Of chief concern was the landing on Howland Island. The patch of land's small size (its highest point was 18 feet, or 5.5 meters) would require a keen set of eyes to land there. It was also 40 miles (64 kilometers) away from the next nearest land, meaning that expert aerial navigation would be needed to ensure a successful landing. Manning expressed complete confidence in his ability to pull off the landing, but Paul Mantz was skeptical. He knew that Manning's expertise was naval navigation rather than aerial navigation. As a result, after some deliberation, it was decided that Fred Noonan, who had served aboard the Pan American Pacific Clipper as a navigator, would be brought in as a second navigator. Noonan's experience in the Pacific and his aerial navigation expertise would come in handy should any problems arise during the flight.

Some controversies, however, came along with Noonan's hiring. The navigator, despite his distinguished service record, had a history of drinking, and rumors persisted that his departure from Pan Am was a result of his problems with alcohol. While the rumors were untrue, the fact that Noonan could not always manage his drinking still posed a problem. His former boss at Pan Am, Clarence L. Schildhauer, recalled Noonan's battles with the bottle, saying that Noonan was "the best navigator when he was sober, but he was inclined to go on benders. . . . Before takeoff he'd have to be hunted down and 'poured' aboard the airplane."[1]

With these concerns in mind, it was ultimately decided to split up the navigation duties. Noonan would travel with Earhart to Howland Island, then Manning would take over to Australia, leaving Earhart to complete the journey on her own.

LEAVING THE GROUND

On March 17, 1937, after several days of bad weather, Earhart took off from Oakland Airport, bound for Hawaii. Not many reporters were present, although one photographer managed to snap a picture of the Electra flying over the still-incomplete Golden Gate Bridge as it made its way west.

On board with Earhart were Mantz, Manning, and Noonan. Mantz was seated at Earhart's right while Manning and Noonan handled navigation duties from a special table bolted into the floor of the plane's cabin.

Fifteen hours and forty-seven minutes after leaving California, the Electra appeared in the skies over Wheeler Field in Honolulu. Earhart, tired from the long trip, turned the landing over to Mantz, who set the plane down easily. Although everyone was eager to continue the trip, fatigue and weather dictated that they delay leaving for one more day. After all, the most difficult task, the journey to Howland Island, awaited them, and it would not do to attempt the landing under anything less than ideal circumstances.

The Electra was transferred from Wheeler Field to Luke Field, where the paved runway would make takeoff much easier, particularly given the fact that Earhart had loaded the plane with 900 gallons (3,400 liters) of fuel, an insurance policy in case the landing at Howland did not go as planned.

The next morning, Earhart, Manning, and Noonan sat on the tarmac in the predawn light awaiting takeoff. Finally, Earhart gave the signal to the ground crew to remove the chocks holding the plane in place. She was ready to take off.

Earhart revved the plane's engines and made her way down the runway, gathering speed as she did. After the plane had traveled about 1,000 feet (305 meters), something went horribly wrong. The plane veered sharply to the right, almost as though it dropped its right wing. Earhart acted quickly, decreasing power on the opposite engine, swinging

Amelia Earhart, with navigator Fred Noonan behind her, emerged from her Electra plane after it crashed on takeoff in March 1937 at Luke Field in Hawaii. The crash delayed Earhart's plans for her around-the-world flight for several months.

the plane over to the left. Unfortunately, this caused the plane to continue spinning to the left in what was known as a ground loop. The out-of-control movement of the plane caused the right wheel and the undercarriage to be ripped away and the plane skidded wildly down the runaway on its belly in a shower of sparks and a river of gasoline.

Earhart calmly cut the engine to prevent an explosion as fire crews raced out to the tarmac. She, Manning, and Noonan emerged from the aircraft shaken but unbowed. Noonan even said on the spot that he would be ready to go again when the word was given. Earhart shared his optimism. The plane was shattered and in need of repair, and the flight would be delayed, but Earhart did not see this as the end. This was only a setback. Before too long, the flight around the world would resume.

PLAN B

The news from the Lockheed factory was not encouraging. Repairs would take up to five weeks, and the replacement of damaged parts would cost $25,000. On top of that, the crash had caused some to call Earhart's ability as a pilot into question. Since it happened in full view of the public and the press, there was no way to hide the crash, no way to cover it up and spin it into good PR. Although Earhart's team tried initially to blame the crash on mechanical failure, most people were not buying it. Major Al Williams, a well-known pilot and a respected name in aviation, blasted Earhart in a newspaper article:

> She lost control of the plane during a takeoff on the concrete runway on a standard Army airdrome and wrecked the "Flying Laboratory." And there again the public got a garbled story and a cleverly contrived explanation . . . plus a heroic story about cutting the switches and saving the lives of her crew. That ship got away from her on the takeoff—that's the low-down.[2]

Nevertheless, Earhart rose above the bad press and set about rethinking her around-the-globe flight. The first order of business was rearranging the route. The March flight had been planned according to optimal weather patterns along the route. With the flight now postponed until May, a new route would have to be worked out. This would cost money, as rerouting the flight also meant making entirely new arrangements for the dispensation of fuel and supplies along the new flight path. Earhart and Putnam hoped that they could recoup some of the flight's costs with a book chronicling the trip, to be written by Earhart and provisionally titled *World Flight*. As she made her preparations for the new flight, Earhart made extensive notes that would serve as the opening chapters of the book. As she traveled, she planned to mail her notes to Putnam, who would have them typed and prepared, ensuring that the book could be published as quickly as possible after the flight.

Shortly after the crash, Manning informed Earhart that he would not be making the flight around the world. He explained to her that it was because his three-month leave of absence from his job would expire before the flight could take place. Years later, though, he admitted that his decision was based on the fact that he had no faith in Earhart's flying ability and had some issues with her personality as well. "Amelia Earhart was something of a prima donna," he said.

> She gave the impression of being humble and shy, but she really had an ego, and could be as tough as nails when the occasion required it. I got very fed up with her bull-headedness several times. . . . AE herself was not a good navigator; and Noonan was a happy-go-lucky Irishman. He wasn't a "constant" navigator.[3]

Manning's departure did not set the flight back, however, and preparations continued. The speed of the preparations concerned Mantz, who believed that plans were moving ahead more quickly than he would have liked. For example, he was stunned to learn that Earhart had opted to remove the emergency radio antenna because she felt it would be too difficult to reel in and out. Radioman Joe Gurr had tried to boost the onboard radio's signal by moving the antenna as far forward on the plane as possible. It was not as good as the trailing wire, but it could work over limited distances. Mantz felt that this gap in communication could create a potentially lethal situation.

Further friction was created when Mantz was not consulted on the new route. Earhart planned to travel from west to east, starting in Oakland and then traveling to Miami. This put the dangerous landing on Howland Island at the end of the trip rather than at the beginning and meant that Noonan would be along for the entire flight.

The last straw came on Thursday, May 21, 1937, when Earhart took off from Oakland bound for Miami without Mantz's knowledge. Mantz and Earhart had been working together in California right until the day before her departure. As far as he knew, she had no plans to leave for a few days, and he opted to go to St. Louis to take part in an aerobatics competition. When he received word that Earhart had departed on what she referred to as a "shakedown" flight to test the Electra, he was furious. Although she claimed the flight was simply a means of putting the plane through its paces, Mantz knew better. He could not believe she would undertake such a dangerous flight in such a foolhardy fashion. There were still tests to be performed, he argued. But Earhart was pushing herself hard to meet Putnam's plans to make money and promote the flight. Mantz was hurt by Earhart's deception and, even years later, became angry whenever the topic was broached.

THE FLIGHT BEGINS

From Oakland, Earhart, Noonan, Putnam, and mechanic Bo McKneely flew to Tucson, Arizona, to refuel. After a short layover, they were preparing to get under way again when the left engine caught fire as soon as Earhart started the plane. The flames were snuffed out by the plane's onboard fire extinguisher system, and McKneely quickly worked to repair the burnt equipment.

While sitting in a hangar in Miami, Florida, in May 1937, Amelia Earhart and George Putnam talked over the plans for Earhart's attempt to fly around the world. She would take off on the journey just days later.

The next morning they set off for New Orleans for an overnight stay before arriving in Miami on May 23. They spent a week there testing and retesting the Electra to ensure its readiness for the flight. Finally, on June 1, everything was ready.

A small crowd gathered in the dawn light to watch Earhart and Noonan leave on their historic flight. Reporters milled about the Electra, snapping photos of Earhart and Putnam holding hands as she sat on the wing of her aircraft. When the crowd had retreated somewhat, the couple sidled off to a hangar for a more private farewell. Recalling this final moment, Putnam later remembered:

There in the dim chill we perched briefly on cold concrete steps, her hands in mine. There is very little one says at such times.

When Bo called that all was ready, Amelia's eyes were clear with the good light of the adventure that lay before her. But as she walked out to the [airplane] she seemed to me very small and slim and feminine.[4]

As the sun came up over the Miami skyline, Earhart revved the engines of the Electra as it slowly made its way upward. Standing on the roof of the airfield's administration building, Putnam watched, pacing nervously as the plane rose higher and higher into the morning sky. Soon it was little more than a silver glint in the Florida sun as it headed to the southeast. George Putnam would never see Amelia Earhart again.

IN HER OWN WORDS

In one of her last conversations with her husband, just before her flight around the world, Amelia Earhart said:

> I know that if I fail or if I am lost, you will be blamed for allowing me to leave on this trip; the backers of the flight will be blamed and everyone connected with it. But it's my responsibility and mine alone.*

* Mary S. Lovell, *The Sound of Wings: The Life of Amelia Earhart.* New York: St. Martin's Press, 1989, p. 258.

CIRCLING THE GLOBE

There was no turning back. Earhart's around-the-world flight was now officially under way, and the whole world was following her. News about the trip splashed across the front pages of newspapers everywhere, and people were glued to their radios listening for any updates that came along.

In the air, the trip was going smoothly. Earhart and Noonan flew 1,000 miles (1,600 kilometers) to San Juan, Puerto Rico. The area was well known to Noonan, and there were no problems whatsoever, boosting Earhart's confidence.

They spent the night with a mutual friend, Clara Livingston, whose dramatic hacienda featured twin stair-cases that led directly to the beach, and then rose at dawn to continue the flight.

They had planned to journey next to Paramaribo in Dutch Guiana, but fuel concerns led to them to shift their itinerary and fly to Caripito, Venezuela. From there, they traveled to Paramaribo and then to Fortaleza in Brazil. Everywhere they went, they were met with goodwill and kind wishes from the local people. In one store in Fortaleza, Noonan attempted to purchase sponge rubber and liquid cement, only to have the proprietor refuse his money and give him the items as a gift.

After resting in Fortaleza briefly, Earhart and Noonan resumed the flight, traveling to Natal, which would serve as a jumping-off point for their trip over the South Atlantic Ocean to Dakar in Senegal, Africa, a flight of about 1,900 miles (3,050 kilometers). Unfortunately, they did not land in Dakar, because Earhart had doubts about Noonan's suggested course. With the African coast obscured by haze, she questioned his notion to turn south and instead turned north, taking them to St. Louis, Senegal.

The next morning, they traveled to Dakar, where they were guests of the governor-general. From Dakar, they traveled to Gao in present-day Mali, where, due to the intense heat, they slept out in the open desert. Leaving Gao, Earhart and Noonan made their way down the Niger River, stopping at El Fasher in the Sudan, where they stayed in the palace of a former sultan. As they flew over Africa, Earhart flashed back to her childhood, remembering her fantasies of travel and exploration. As places with such exotic names as Qala-en Hahl, Umm Shinayshin, and Timbuktu passed below their plane, she could not help but feel delighted. She was truly living out her dreams.

Navigation over Africa proved difficult for Noonan, as there were few maps and those that were available were not always reliable. Nevertheless, they managed to hold their course with few troubles and soon were making their way down the Red Sea to Assab in Eritrea, and then along the Arabian coastline to India. In doing so, Earhart set another record, as no one had ever made a nonstop flight from the Red Sea to India.

In Karachi, the Electra's fuel analyzer was replaced, thanks to instructions cabled from Putnam. In addition, ace pilot Jacques de Sibour was waiting for them with new maps and data that would help them navigate their way much more easily. Earhart also managed to talk with Putnam during her stay in Karachi, telling him what a good time she was having and saying that the two of them should make this trip together sometime.

From Karachi, the Electra flew to Calcutta, arriving there in the wake of a tremendous rainfall that had left the airfield soaked and muddy. With more rain in the forecast, Earhart decided to take off immediately and head for Burma (today known as the Union of Myanmar). They did not get far, however, as the monsoon-like torrent forced them down in Akyab. They took off the next morning

Amelia Earhart and navigator Fred Noonan relaxed shortly after their land-ing on June 21, 1937, in Bandoeng, in what is now Indonesia. Because of repairs and bad weather, the two remained in Bandoeng for several days. Earhart used the time to take in a few local sights.

but again had to land in Rangoon. After the weather cleared, Earhart and Noonan made their way to Bangkok, Singapore, and Bandoeng in the Dutch East Indies, where repairs and weather led to a stay of several days. During this time Earhart became something of a tourist, taking in the local sights and dishes and purchasing souvenirs for friends back home. Unfortunately, her sampling of the food led to a rather devastating case of dysentery. She also found time to talk with Putnam again, informing him that the flight was progressing excellently and that she expected to be home by the Fourth of July.

Eventually, Earhart's health cleared up and the Electra was repaired, allowing them to leave on June 27 for Port Darwin, Australia. After arriving there, Earhart and Noonan discovered that a fuse had blown on the direction finder and needed to be replaced. While there, the Electra's parachutes were offloaded and shipped back to the United States. The next leg of the journey would take them over the Pacific and, should they run into trouble there, Earhart argued, parachutes would not do them any good.

THE PACIFIC

The 1,200-mile (1,930-kilometer) journey from Port Darwin to Lae, Papua New Guinea, took Earhart and Noonan 7 hours, 43 minutes to complete. They were now in the homestretch. Only 7,000 miles (11,265 kilometers) separated them from their home. But they still had to cross the wide expanse of the Pacific Ocean.

In New Guinea, they worked feverishly to get the Electra prepped for this, the most dangerous leg of the flight. Any excess weight was removed, the fuel pump and the autopilot were repaired, spark plugs were cleaned, and the oil filters were changed.

It had been more than a month since Earhart had left Oakland, and it showed in her face. She looked tired and drawn with puffy, sleep-deprived eyes. It is not surprising, given the rigors of the trip. Besides the duties of flying the plane, Earhart had also visited with dignitaries in nearly every city they stopped in, spoke with reporters, wrote close to 30,000 words for her book, and published a series of articles in the *Herald Tribune*, which were later compiled into a book entitled *Last Flight*. In one of those articles, she gives some insight into her mind-set at the outset of the last leg of the journey:

> Not much more than a month ago I was on the other shore of the Pacific, looking westward. This evening, I look eastward over the Pacific. In those fast-moving days which have intervened, the whole width of the world had passed behind us—except this broad ocean. I shall be glad when we have the hazards of its navigation behind us.[5]

Before leaving for Howland Island, Earhart made some adjustments to the flight plan, opting to redirect the flight over the island of Narau (now known as Nauru). Phosphate mining operations on the island generated constant light, even at night, which would make spotting the island from the air very easy. The island also lay almost 1,400 miles (2,250 kilometers) into the 2,556-mile (4,113-kilometer) flight to Howland.

Earhart figured the flight would take approximately 18 hours, some of which would have to be at night to guarantee a crucial daylight landing on Howland. That meant that a proper departure time from Lae would have to be settled on. In addition, the plane would cross the International Date Line and two time zones, which would make receiving communications from the Coast Guard cutter *Itasca*, which ran on Navy Time, more difficult. Taking these factors into account, Noonan made the decision to take off at 00:00 Greenwich Mean Time, which would mean that the time of their flight would match the time on the chronometers, regardless of time zones. For example, if they were in the air for 14 hours, the chronometer would read 14:00 GMT. It seemed to be the most logical solution to the time-zone problem.

With everything taken care of and all major problems addressed, Earhart and Noonan climbed into the Electra on July 2, 1937. It was 10 A.M. local time, and the morning was already blisteringly hot, so much so that the metal skin of the Electra was hot to the touch. But the air was clear, and it was time to fly. The plane made its way down the 1,000-yard (914-meter) runway and took off over the waters of the Huon Gulf, heading out to the sea. It was the last time anyone would ever see Amelia Earhart.

Legacy

For nearly eight hours into the flight, Amelia Earhart kept steady radio contact with Lae, talking to Harry Balfour, a radio operator for New Guinea Airways. According to these radio transmissions, Earhart and Fred Noonan were on course, but were making less time than expected. At their present speed, it was calculated, it would take Earhart and Noonan another 13 hours to reach Howland.

In the sea, all eyes were on the sky. The Coast Guard cutter USS *Ontario* was designated as Earhart's guard ship along the Lae-Howland route, and the men on board were keeping a watchful eye for the Electra. Earhart had instructed the *Ontario*'s captain to broadcast the letter "N" via Morse code for five minutes after every hour with the ship's call letters to follow. However, after 10 hours of broadcasting and watching the sky, Earhart's plane was not seen. Two hours after the Electra was due to pass overhead, the *Ontario* received orders to return to port for supplies.

Meanwhile, the Coast Guard cutter *Itasca*, painted bright white, was lying just off the northeastern end of Howland Island. The ship was sending up black smoke as a signal that could be seen for miles. The skies were clear and visibility was good, but there was no sign of Earhart. Finally, at 14:15 hours GMT, the ship received a faint transmission from Earhart's plane. No one could make out exactly what she was saying, but *Itasca* radioman Leo G. Bellarts claimed he could make out the words "cloudy and overcast." For the next hour, they heard nothing until 15:15 hours, when she broadcast again, this time much clearer, informing the *Itasca* that conditions were still overcast. The ship radioed back, asking for the Electra's position, but received no response.

SCANNING THE SKIES

Over the next hour and 20 minutes, Bellarts continued to send weather data and request the Electra's position but received no reply. Finally, 17 hours into the flight, a clear signal came through, indicating that Earhart was close. She reported that she was approximately 200 miles (322 kilometers) out and was going to whistle into the microphone in order for the ship to get a bearing on her. Unfortunately, the whistle was lost in a barrage of static, and the radio operators could not get a fixed position on Earhart. About a half hour later, 15 minutes or so past the time she was due to arrive at Howland Island, Earhart was heard again, this time claiming she was approximately 100 miles (161 kilometers) out. Once again she suggested whistling into the microphone in order for the *Itasca* to pinpoint her location. This time, however, her whistle was too brief for the ship to locate her.

More than 19 hours after leaving Lae, Earhart came in again over the radio, this time at the maximum volume, indicating that she must be close by. According to Bellarts's log, her transmission was as follows: "We must be on you but cannot see you but gas running low. Been unable to reach you by radio. We are flying at altitude 1,000 feet."[1]

Some reports have the transmission as reading, "running out of gas, only half an hour left," while the ship's secondary log says, "Earhart says running out of gas. Only half an hour left/can't hear us at all/we hear her and are sending on 3105 and 500 same time constantly and listening in for her frequently."[2] Whatever the case was, it was clear that Earhart's situation was quickly becoming dire.

Aware of the gravity of the circumstances, the *Itasca* began to send a constant series of transmissions on two separate frequencies. Finally, they heard from Earhart, who confirmed what those aboard had most likely feared, that she had received their radio messages but could not locate the ship. Again, she asked that a bearing be taken on her, but again the message was too brief.

Now the crew aboard the *Itasca* kicked their efforts into overdrive, with Bellarts broadcasting voice and code messages on every frequency the Electra was capable of receiving. He continued to do this for more than a half hour, but heard no reply. At last, 20 hours and 14 minutes into the flight, Earhart's voice came over the radio. Although the signal was strong, it was not as loud as earlier transmissions. Reports from the *Itasca* have suggested that Earhart sounded under stress and somewhat disjointed. According to the ship's logs, she said: "KHAQQ to *Itasca*. We are on the line of position one five seven dash three three seven. Will repeat this message on 6120 kilocycles. We are running north and south."[3]

Bellarts replied immediately, asking that she stay on the same frequency and not repeat the message on a different one, but he received no reply. He continued to send transmissions for more than an hour, but there was no reply. Nothing was ever heard from Amelia Earhart again.

LOST

After an hour of trying to raise the Electra via radio, Commander Warner Thompson, captain of the *Itasca*, came to the conclusion that Earhart had run out of fuel and been forced to ditch in the ocean. He immediately began to initiate a search procedure. He ordered the vessel to head north, basing his decision on Earhart's last transmissions. Given that she was flying under 1,000 feet (305 meters), Thompson concluded that she had to be flying below a cloudbank. These clouds could also have prevented her from seeing the plume of black smoke sent up by the ship.

The search effort produced no trace of the Electra or its crew. It was July 2, 1937, 22 days before her fortieth birthday. Amelia Earhart was gone.

THE SEARCH

Most successful rescues at sea occur within the first 24 hours. With that in mind, all the people involved in the search for Earhart had to accept a harsh truth: Time was not on their side.

Over the next 16 days, the world sat riveted as the largest search-and-rescue attempt ever made for one aircraft was undertaken. More than 250,000 square miles (647,500 square kilometers) were searched by 65 airplanes, 10 ships, and 4,000 men. Ships were even sent from Britain and Japan. The fastest aircraft carrier in the American naval fleet, the USS *Lexington*, was dispatched from Santa Barbara, California, almost immediately after putting into port.

Meanwhile, radio operators on the mainland kept everyone's hopes alive by reporting that they had picked up radio signals from the Electra. Walter McMenamy, a Los

Sitting at a Coast Guard radio station in San Francisco with maps and charts, George Putnam assisted in the search for Amelia Earhart the day after her disappearance on July 2, 1937. The search-and-rescue mission to locate Earhart's plane lasted 16 days and was the largest ever undertaken for one aircraft.

Angeles-based radio operator who had kept radio contact with Earhart during her solo Pacific flight two years earlier, claimed that he had picked up faint Morse code signals on the 6120 kilocycle frequency used by Earhart's Electra. Later, he reported having heard her voice calling out, "SOS, SOS, SOS."

George Putnam, never one to sit idly by, personally oversaw the rescue effort, scanning charts and maps for probable locations where Earhart could have landed and communicating with the navy regarding new places to search.

Eventually, however, all those involved came to the same grim conclusion: The search was fruitless, and the chances that Earhart and Noonan would be found had grown impossibly slim. On July 18, 1937, the search was officially abandoned.

Putnam did not give up as easily. He continued to try to rally support for further searching and, in the interest of

THE MYSTERY SOLVED?

Although nothing official has ever been announced, research-ers at The International Group for Historic Aircraft Recovery (TIGHAR) are convinced that they have conclusively solved the riddle of Amelia Earhart's disappearance.

In 1940, just three years after the Electra was reported lost, a British Colonial Service officer named Gerald Gallagher found a partially decomposed skeleton on Nikumaroro Island, which lies approximately 300 miles (483 kilometers) southeast of Howland Island. Although these bones were lost over time, TIGHAR researchers have used this discovery as evidence that Earhart did not crash in the ocean but may have survived and lived as a castaway for some time after the fact. Other items found near the bones—a woman's shoe, an empty bottle, and a sextant box with serial numbers consistent with Noonan's equipment—also help to bolster the argument. "The evidence is plentiful—but not conclusive yet—to support the hypothesis that Amelia landed and died on the island of Nikumaroro,"* Karen Ramey Burns, a forensic anthropologist, explained in an interview with Discovery News.

TIGHAR members also point to the search effort itself, not-ing that Lt. John O. Lambrecht, a U.S. naval aviator, flew over Nikumaroro and reported evidence of habitation on what was

keeping Earhart's name alive, arranged for the notes from her journey to be compiled into a book, *Last Flight*. The book arrived on shelves in November 1937 and proved to be a modest success.

As time went on, Putnam met another woman, Jean-Marie Cosigny James, and the two, after a brief courtship, fell in love. For him to marry Jeannie (as he called her),

supposedly an abandoned island. Given the island's small size, it is feasible that, had Earhart even been there, flagging the plane down wildly, she might not have been seen.

Nikumaroro is a dangerous and inhospitable island, with temperatures that reach well into the 100s (more than 38°C). Chances are great that, had Earhart and Noonan been stranded there, they would have quickly succumbed to the island's unforgiving climate, dying of dehydration, starvation, or possibly infection due to injuries sustained in the crash. The island is also home to swarms of coconut crabs that would have quickly consumed the bodies of the aviators, leaving little or no trace. As for the Electra, the strong waves that pound the shores of Nikumaroro would have torn the craft to pieces and whisked it away to deep waters, where it still may lie today.

As of 2011, TIGHAR still makes expeditions to Nikumaroro, combing the island extensively for any trace of Earhart. One day, perhaps not too long from now, the mystery of the pioneering flier might be finally laid to rest.

---

* Rossella Lorenzi, "Earhart's Final Resting Place Believed Found." Discovery News, October 23, 2009. http://news.discovery.com/history/amelia-earhart-resting-place.html.

certain legal proceedings needed to be undertaken, specifically those regarding his marriage to Earhart. In general, a person cannot be declared legally dead until he or she has been missing for seven years. Putnam's attorneys, however, argued that Earhart's circumstances were different. The world had witnessed the search for her firsthand, and testimony from those involved would conclusively prove to the courts that Earhart could not possibly have survived. And so it was that, on January 5, 1939, George Putnam had his wife declared legally dead. Although no body was ever found, on paper at least, the bold and daring life of Amelia Earhart had officially come to an end.

ENDURING ICON

These days, when Amelia Earhart's name is mentioned, the talk turns to the legends and theories surrounding her disappearance more than the achievements she made during her brief but prosperous career. Some say she was actually on a spy mission for President Franklin Roosevelt and was captured and executed by the Japanese. Others claim that she was captured by the Japanese and forced to serve as Tokyo Rose, one of several English-speaking women who broadcast Japanese propaganda to Allied forces during World War II. This particular theory was of interest to

DID YOU KNOW?

The creators of the hit TV series *Lost,* which took place on a mysterious uncharted South Pacific island, added their own twist to the Amelia Earhart legend by giving one of its characters, an elderly woman who had lived on the island for a long time, the name Amelia.

The disappearance of Amelia Earhart often overshadows her accomplishments as a pioneering aviator. She defied expectations and conventions and continues to serve as a role model to this day.

Putnam, who listened to recordings of various Tokyo Roses but could find none that he felt matched Earhart's voice. Another (wholly false) claim was that Earhart survived the flight and moved to New Jersey, living out the rest of her days as Irene Craigmile Bolam. This claim was thoroughly discredited when Bolam was able to produce solid, irrefutable documentation proving that she could not possibly be the famous aviatrix.

But all the wild speculation surrounding Earhart's probable death should not overshadow the events of her life. In only a few short years, Earhart redefined what a woman was capable of. She defied the conventions of society and became a role model for women's achievement. She cherished her place as a role model and used her fame and influence to further women's causes, creating groups like the Ninety-Nines, that continue to flourish today.

Amelia Earhart was more than a feminist, however. She harbored no greater agenda than simply proving that she could achieve the goals she set for herself and become what she wanted to be regardless of any limits society or culture placed on her. Her triumphs in aviation are legendary, but her impact on society as a whole is no less important. Though she may be gone from this world, the spirit of Amelia Earhart lives on in any person who looks out to the horizon and dreams that, despite their circumstances, they can fly higher.

CHRONOLOGY

1897   Amelia Earhart is born on July 24 in
        Atchison, Kansas, to Edwin Stanton and
        Amy Otis Earhart.

1908   Amelia attends the Iowa State Fair, where
        she sees her first airplane.

1917   Serves as a nurse's aide in a Canadian
        hospital during World War I.

1920   Moves to California and takes her first
        flight.

1921   Begins to take flying lessons under Neta
        Snook.

1922   Sets an unofficial air record, becoming the
        first woman to fly at 14,000 feet (4,267
        meters).

1924   Moves back to the East Coast.

1925   Becomes a social worker at Denison
        House, a settlement house in Boston.

1928   Flies across the Atlantic Ocean aboard the
        Friendship. Becomes the first woman to
        complete a transcontinental flight.

1931   Marries George Putnam.

1932   Flies solo across the Atlantic Ocean and is
        awarded the Distinguished Flying Cross
        from the U.S. Congress. Becomes the
        first woman to fly solo nonstop across the
        United States.

1935   Makes the first-ever solo flight across the
        Pacific Ocean, flying from Honolulu to
        Oakland, California. Accepts a position

as a lecturer and consultant at Purdue University.

1936   Begins to make plans for a flight around the world.

1937   Makes her first attempt at an around-the-world flight, leaving from Oakland, California, and setting a record for east-west travel from California to Hawaii. Departs from Miami on her second attempt. Disappears while flying to Howland Island in the Pacific Ocean on July 2.

1939   Court declares her legally dead on January 5.

NOTES

CHAPTER 3

1. Mary S. Lovell, *The Sound of Wings: The Life of Amelia Earhart*. New York: St. Martin's Press, 1989, p. 25.
2. Susan Butler, *East to the Dawn: The Life of Amelia Earhart*. Philadelphia: Da Capo Press, 1999, p. 83.
3. Amelia Earhart, *20 Hrs., 40 Min.: Our Flight in the Friendship*. Washington, D.C.: National Geographic Society, 2003, pp. 3–4.
4. Lovell, *The Sound of Wings*, p. 26.
5. Butler, *East to the Dawn*, p. 85.
6. Lovell, *The Sound of Wings*, p. 28.
7. Earhart, *20 Hrs., 40 Min.*, p. 8.
8. Lovell, *The Sound of Wings*, p. 29.

CHAPTER 4

1. Earhart, *20 Hrs., 40 Min.*, pp. 12–13.
2. Lovell, *The Sound of Wings*, p. 32.
3. Donald M. Goldstein and Katherine V. Dillon, *Amelia: A Life of the Aviation Legend*. Dulles, Va.: Potomac Books, 1997, p. 31.
4. Lovell, *The Sound of Wings*, pp. 33–34.
5. Earhart, *20 Hrs., 40 Min.*, p. 14.
6. Butler, *East to the Dawn*, p. 103.
7. Ibid., p. 103.
8. Earhart, *20 Hrs., 40 Min.*, p. 23.
9. Butler, *East to the Dawn*, p. 105.
10. Earhart, *20 Hrs., 40 Min.*, p. 15.
11. Ibid., pp. 16–17.
12. Ibid., p. 17.

CHAPTER 5

1. Earhart, *20 Hrs., 40 Min.*, p. 27.
2. Ibid., p. 28.

3. Ibid., p. 29.
4. Lovell, *The Sound of Wings*, p. 31.
5. Butler, *East to the Dawn*, p. 134.
6. Ibid., p. 138.
7. Ibid., p. 151.
8. Ibid., p. 153.
9. Earhart, *20 Hrs., 40 Min.*, pp. 40–41.

CHAPTER 6

1. Earhart, *20 Hrs., 40 Min.*, p. 43.
2. Ibid., p. 46.
3. Ibid., p. 46.
4. Ibid., pp. 58–61.
5. Ibid., p. 65.

CHAPTER 7

1. Lovell, *The Sound of Wings*, p. 123.
2. Ibid., p. 124.
3. Ibid., p. 136.
4. Butler, *East to the Dawn*, p. 251.

CHAPTER 8

1. Lovell, *The Sound of Wings*, p. 170.
2. Ibid., p. 178.
3. Ibid., p. 179.
4. Ibid., p. 180.
5. Ibid., p. 181.
6. Butler, *East to the Dawn*, p. 270.
7. "About All She Has Proved," *New York Post*, May 21, 1932. http://earchives.lib.purdue.edu/cdm4/item_ viewer.php?CISOROOT=/earhart&CISOPTR=320 0&CISOBOX=1&REC=6.

CHAPTER 9

1. Lovell, *The Sound of Wings*, p. 206.
2. Butler, *East to the Dawn*, p. 328.
3. Ibid., p. 333.

CHAPTER 10

1. Lovell, *The Sound of Wings*, pp. 242–243.
2. Ibid., p. 249.
3. Ibid., p. 252.
4. Ibid., p. 259.
5. Ibid., p. 265.

CHAPTER 11

1. Butler, *East to the Dawn*, p. 409.
2. Lovell, *The Sound of Wings*, p. 280.
3. Ibid., p. 282.

BIBLIOGRAPHY

Butler, Susan. *East to the Dawn: The Life of Amelia Earhart.* Philadelphia: Da Capo Press, 1999.

Earhart, Amelia. *20 Hrs., 40 Min.: Our Flight in the Friendship.* Washington, D.C.: National Geographic Society, 2003.

Goldstein, Donald M., and Katherine V. Dillon. *Amelia: A Life of the Aviation Legend.* Dulles, Va.: Potomac Books, 1997.

Long, Elgen M., and Marie K. Long. *Amelia Earhart: The Mystery Solved.* New York: Simon & Schuster, 1999.

Lovell, Mary S. *The Sound of Wings: The Life of Amelia Earhart.* New York: St. Martin's Press, 1989.

Wagner, Heather Lehr. *Amelia Earhart.* Philadelphia: Chelsea House Publishers, 2003.

FURTHER RESOURCES

BOOKS

Burns, Karen Ramey. *Amelia Earhart's Shoes: Is the Mystery Solved?* Lanham, Md.: AltaMira Press, 2004.

Butler, Sue, Kristen Lubben, and Erin Barnett. *Amelia Earhart: Image and Icon*. London: Steidl/International Center of Photography, 2007.

Grant, R.G. *Flight: 100 Years of Aviation*. New York: DK Publishing, 2007.

Marck, Bernard. *Women Aviators: From Amelia Earhart to Sally Ride, Making History in Air and Space*. Paris: Flammarion, 2009.

Winters, Kathleen C. *Amelia Earhart: The Turbulent Life of an American Icon*. New York: Palgrave Macmillan, 2010.

WEB SITES

Amelia Earhart Birthplace Museum
http://www.ameliaearhartmuseum.org/

Amelia Earhart: The Official Website
http://www.ameliaearhart.com

George Palmer Putnam Collection of Amelia Earhart Papers
http://www.lib.purdue.edu/spcol/aearhart/

The International Group for Historic Aircraft Recovery
http://tighar.org/

The Ninety-Nines Inc., International Organization of Women Pilots
http://www.ninety-nines.org/

PICTURE CREDITS

INDEX

ABOUT THE AUTHOR

JEREMY K. BROWN has written for numerous magazines and publications, including *Star, Country Music Today, Wizard, Current Biography,* and *WWE Magazine.* He is the editor of the reference book *Warfare in the 21st Century* and has also authored *Ursula K. Le Guin* and *Stevie Wonder* for Chelsea House. He lives in New York with his family.